The Pioneer Z

America's First Diesel-Electric Stainless Steel Streamliner

Burlington Route

Carl R. Byron

With Robert W. Rediske

With Special Acknowledgment to

The late Robert W. Rediske

for his unique, first-person account of the world's record passenger train speed run between Denver and Chicago on May 26, 1934. Mr. Rediske was the last survivor of that famous record-setting trip.

Acknowledgments

Wallace W. Abby, whose advice and counsel have been invaluable in setting the tone of the early streamline era: "She Sure is Coming—Wasn't She."; Donald J. Heimburger, Heimburger House Publishing Co., without whose encouragement and commitment this book would not have been possible; Sally King, archivist, BNSF Railway, for permission to reproduce the photographs of the Zephyr from the BNSF archives; Andy Zakrajsek, director of retail businesses and Lindsey MacAllister, archivist, Museum of Science and Industry, who opened the Museum's archives for the research necessary to create this book; Rick Nowell, archivist, Boston & Maine Railroad Historical Society, Inc., for permission to reproduce B&M Manager E. K. Bloss's report on the Zephyr's initial service.

Also, thanks to Kenneth Bird, Scott Brownell, Chris Burritt, Bernard Golias, J. Michael Gruber, Jim Kindraka and Dan Navarre/River Raisin Models, Robert McGonigal/Kalmbach Publishing, Philip Weibler and Chuck Zeiler.

Photographs and illustrations not identified are from the Museum of Science and Industry archives.

ISBN: 0-911581-58-8
Library of Congress Control Number: 2005925523
Printed in Hong Kong

Covers. The #9900 four-car Pioneer Zephyr resides today at Chicago's Museum of Science and Industry on the lakefront. These photos show the stainless steel train on display at the Museum. *Both photos by Scott Brownell*

Heimburger House Publishing Company
7236 W. Madison Street
Forest Park, Illinois 60130

Table of Contents

On the eve of its millionth mile, the four-car Pioneer Zephyr looks as shiny and polished as the day it began operations in 1934. The seats in the cab for the engineer and fireman were separated by the main generator.

ALL ABOARD!
The God of the West Wind beckons.

The Pioneer Zephyr, God of the West Wind, was an exhilarating breath of fresh air in the midst of the Great Depression. Completed in April of 1934 by the Budd Company of Philadelphia, the Pioneer Zephyr symbolized everything new and modern in rail transportation in America.

Swift, Stylish, and oh, so Sophisticated, the diesel-electric powered stainless steel streamliner arrived on the North American railroad scene April 18, 1934. A breath of exhilarating fresh air in the midst of the Great Depression, it was the first sign that "things would get better."

"Get better" they did, and for the next quarter century the diesel-electric stainless steel streamliner was at the forefront of land transportation, initially setting speed records, but more importantly duly establishing itself as a pleasant, speedy and most civilized mode of land travel.

By the mid-1960s the streamliner era was in eclipse, retreating under the combined assault of the speed of the jet aircraft and the convenience of the automobile. Still, for more than three decades the combination of internal combustion, electric drive and stainless steel produced a mode of travel worthy of remembrance.

Symbolized Streamline Era

There were, of course, streamliners welded or riveted from carbon steel or aluminum, and powered by electric or steam motive power such as the Southern Pacific *Daylights*, the Union Pacific *City* trains, or the Pennsylvania Fleet of Modernism. Still, glistening Shotwelded stainless steel cars trailing brightly-painted diesel-electric locomotives powering the likes of the Santa Fe *Super Chief*, the Canadian Pacific *Canadian*, or the Burlington Route *Denver Zephyr* seemed to best symbolize the streamline era.

It all started with a diminutive 104-ton, 3-car Zephyr powered by an eight-cylinder Winton diesel engine producing 660 gross horsepower. A saga of desperation, determination and innovation, it could be an Horatio Alger "All American" tall tale. However, it is true—and must be—for no novelist could have envisioned the twists and turns of this uniquely American industrial and historical adventure.

Now, lean back in your comfortable seat and relax as our Zephyr departs for distant points. No need to worry about traffic jams, fogged or snowed-in airports, or crowded restaurants and hotels. Soon it will be "First call for dinner" in the diner, nothing could be finer. Sleep will come beneath snowy white sheets surrounded by sturdy stainless steel tested to deflect no more than 1/4" under 1 million pounds of force. The post-1960 generations raised on burger and pizza shop drive-through window service, and airliners utilizing 11-abreast seating, haven't a clue as to how true the great Cunard Steamship Line's advertising slogan, "Getting there is half the fun," once was.

— Prologue —

American railroads dominated land transportation during the first quarter of the 20th Century. By any measure, from track miles to passenger volume or financial chicanery, the railroads entered the 20th Century with their robber baron image intact and at least partially justified.

It was the height of the Steam and Steel Era. Coal-fired steam locomotives of ever-increasing size and power were being built to haul freight and passenger trains of growing length and weight.

From the earliest days of American railroading rolling stock had been constructed of wood. However, several early 20th Century accidents involving large numbers of fatalities due to the tragic combination of fire and the "telescoping" of wooden passenger cars one into another led to the introduction of steel passenger equipment in 1907. Industry-wide conversion to steel cars was hastened by the Pennsylvania RR's refusal to handle wooden cars through its new Pennsylvania Station and associated Hudson and East River tunnels into New York City.

The Pullman Company

Although most coaches or chair cars were railroad owned, virtually all the sleeping cars and many of the dining and parlor cars plying American rails were owned and operated by the Pullman Company of Chicago. George M. Pullman founded his company circa 1860, and by 1900 Pullman had a monopoly on the nationwide operation of sleeping cars. Its influence was so pervasive that a small traveling case introduced during the 1920's for ladies to carry their overnight essentials in was quickly dubbed a "Pullman." More than 80 years later the case still is a staple for overnight travelers.

The average Pullman car stretched 85' and weighed between 75 and 85 tons. By the early 1920's through train lengths of 12-15 cars were common, requiring steam locomotives that were ever more destructive to the rails and track structure than their lighter and slower predecessors. Of even more concern, since only 5-7% of the thermal energy contained within the coal fuel used in most steam locomotives actually produced drawbar pull at the coupler end of the tender, the magnificent steam locomotive was an incredible 93-95% inefficient.

Long before the Great Depression enveloped the United States in late 1929, both the steam locomotive and the heavy Pullman cars it pulled so magnificently were ripe for replacement.

New Technology Rises

While steam locomotion was the power of choice for America's railroads, a new and exciting technology was rising from the laboratories and inventive genius of men such as Thomas Edison, Frank Sprague, George Westinghouse and Nikola Tesla. Between 1880 and 1900 they not only began the wholesale electric lighting of American cities, but introduced electric motors for industrial and propulsion applications as well.

The early 1890's found direct current generators, traction motors, distribution systems and switch gear adequately developed to power the trolley and interurban era. Through World War One the copper wires would expand from town to town across America, giving millions of citizens an option to the steam train for local service and—especially in the Midwest—intercity travel as well. Only the combination of Ford's Flivver and paved roads in the 1920's would derail the fleets of trolley and interurban cars.

Concurrent with the late 19th Century electrical geniuses, other experimenters were developing the liquid-fueled internal combustion engine. In 1879 German Nikolaus Otto produced the first four-stroke cycle design engine (intake, compression, ignition/power and exhaust), and a rudimentary prime mover was available for the soon-to-develop auto industry. By 1900 fellow German Karl Benz—who named his new automobile after his niece, Mercedes—and Henry Ford, among hundreds of others, began the long process of putting Western civilization in general—and America in particular—on rubber tires, not flanged wheels.

The price and volatility of gasoline conspired against its use to power large vehicles, including locomotives. However, the heavy oil remaining from a barrel of crude oil after the gasoline and naphtha had been "cracked off" contained sub-

The Chicago, Burlington & Quincy first operated in 1850 when the line between Chicago and Aurora, Illinois was opened. This very early #9 high-stepping steam locomotive was built in the CB&Q's Aurora shops. *Don Heimburger collection*

CB&Q #5622 4-8-4 is an example of modern steam power used on the railroad prior to diesels and streamlining.

stantial energy, was much safer than gasoline since it didn't vaporize under normal conditions and was inexpensive, as there was little use for it other than for treating road surfaces.

Rudolph Diesel began experimenting with an internal combustion engine in Munich, Germany in the early 1890's. Based on Otto's four-stroke cycle design, this so-called "heat engine" used increased compression pressure within the cylinder itself to raise the air trapped within to above the ignition temperature of the fuel. Injection of the liquid fuel occurred just before the piston reached top dead center, and instantaneous ignition occurred without the use of a spark plug.

Because of the substantial energy available in the inexpensive heavy fuel oil the new diesel engine could burn, diesel prime movers were promptly installed in industrial, pipeline pumping, or remote power generating stations. These engines were large bore, long piston travel, and low RPM—several hundred at best—prime movers. Still, their power output could be prodigious, as the 1912 installation of a 12,000 horsepower diesel engine in a German Navy vessel shows. Although the Zephyr's power plant wouldn't materialize for two more decades, the process was now under way.

By the early 1920's the railroads' dominance of land transportation was crumbling. Since the century began, electric trolleys, and particularly the heavier interurban systems, had been annually siphoning off increasing volumes of local busi-

ness. Even more devastating was the construction of seemingly endless miles of paved roads to handle Henry Ford's Flivver and its innumerable siblings. Local passenger traffic dropped by well over 50% in many locations between 1915 and 1925. Still, complete elimination of the money losing steam-powered 2-to-5 car locals was impossible, as operation "in the public interest" was mandated by the Interstate Commerce Commission.

Harold L. Hamilton viewed this financial and operational quagmire as an opportunity. While a White (brand) truck sales manager, Hamilton conceived of a self-propelled rail car as just the ticket to replace the steam-powered locals on these innumerable runs across America.

Self-Propelled Cars

Self-propelled cars were nothing new: the gas-mechanical McKeen car had been puttering around Union Pacific branch lines since 1905. However, early self-propelled cars either used a small steam engine or a gasoline engine with a mechanical transmission. Most were little more than a bus or truck body on flanged wheels, or an interurban car without a trolley pole. They lacked power, the mechanical transmissions were prone to reoccurring failure, rode as if they were bouncing on the ties themselves, and disintegrated if they hit something or derailed. Still, the economics of a two-man crew and a lightweight car were undeniable; motor car operation cost approximated 50% or less of that of steam locomotives.

Hamilton had a ready market—if he could bring a new and more reliable self-propelled car to it.

Hamilton envisioned his cars being fabricated in a regional passenger car builder's shop, such as St. Louis Car in the Midwest, or Osgood Bradley in central New England. A 175-200 hp gasoline engine would power the car by being directly connected to a direct current generator, not to a mechanical transmission. DC power from the generator would feed two traction motors in the front trucks geared to the individual axle sets. Although the car body would be from one subcontractor, the gasoline engine from another, and the DC generator, traction motors and controls from a third, Hamilton's company alone would guarantee the entire railcar package—including minimum performance specifications—to the purchasing railroad.

Thus Harold Hamilton and Paul Turner founded The Electro-Motive Engineering Company in a small Cleveland, Ohio storefront on August 31, 1922. It soon began purchasing gasoline engines from a fellow Cleveland firm, the Winton Engine Company, which had been installing gas or diesel engines in Lake Erie yachts since the mid-teens and diesel-electric yacht drives since 1919.

Successful Demonstration

The two firms complemented each other, and in 1924 the now renamed Electro-Motive Company had two of its gas-electric cars successfully demonstrated and sold: the Chicago Great Western's M-300 and the Great Northern's B-3. Just as Hamilton had envisioned, the plucky little coach/baggage/(and sometimes) RPO combination cars proved more reliable than the steam locomotives they replaced. Many cars operated with a trailer in tow, and the more powerful cars were capable of regularly pulling one or two full-sized steel coaches. Gas electrics saved the roads between 40% and 60% in operating and crew costs over their steam-powered predecessors, and had sootless exhaust as well.

Soon EMC was working with Winton and railroad mechanical departments to repower and return to profitable service older gas-mechanical or steam-powered cars whose unreliable operation had sidelined them. Small gas-electric locomotives were also developed, either directly by EMC/Winton, or built by various railroad backshops with EMC/Winton's assistance. The 175 hp in-line 6-cylinder gas engine grew to a substantial 400 horsepower V-8 within five years.

Although there were other rail car builders and engine suppliers in the field, by the end of the 1920's EMC/Winton's reliable products and excellent field service had earned them about 85% of the nationwide railcar market.

The gas-electric market began to stagnate as the price of gasoline inched upward to $.15 per gallon in the late 1920's. At that price the prodigious appetite of a 300-or-400 hp gasoline engine for fuel made the car nearly as expensive to operate as a steam locomotive. Before a solution to that problem could be developed, the Great Depression arrived and what few orders remained quickly dried up.

Art Deco

The death of Britain's Queen Victoria in 1901 closed the so-called Victorian Age. Its successor was established by 1910: the Art Deco era. Worldwide in scope, with numerous influences from tribal Africa to Egyptian tomb graphics, Art Deco ruled the decorative art world for three decades until the outbreak of World War II.

One component of the Art Deco movement was the so-called stream-line, or moderne school, which decreed objects should have smooth, flowing surfaces presenting the illusion of movement, even when standing still. The rise of aeronautical engineering in the mid-1920s and '30's had substantial influence on this school of design.

The earliest stream-line railroad passenger car design was by one Frederick Adams who tested his concepts on the Baltimore & Ohio Railroad in May and June of 1900. A photograph of Adams' "Wind Splitter" train atop the famous Thomas Viaduct shows wooden cars with fluted sides, nearly flush windows, and a curved, boat-tail observation.

Following Adams' experiments the smooth air-flow design concept lay fallow for several years. In 1905 Union Pacific Chief Mechanical Officer William McKeen developed a knife-prowed, gasoline-engine powered, direct drive motorcar. Initially successful at reducing the cost of branch line operations, the Union Pacific purchased a number of these semi-streamlined self-propelled cars. McKeen subsequently set up an independent company that ultimately sold about 150 of the cars nationwide.

Retrofitted Power Plants

Unfortunately the McKeen Car's primitive chain and clutch drive, as well as its underpowered and failure-prone gasoline engine, sidetracked most of the cars by the mid-teens at the latest. However, beginning in 1925 a number of them were removed from storage behind the local road's backshops and retrofitted with new EMC/Winton gas-electric power plants and new front trucks equipped with traction motors. Then they again started paying their way—at least until the Great Depression intervened.

The Chicago Great Western Railroad in 1929 claimed it created "the world's first stream-line train" from three castoff McKeen cars in its Oelwein, Iowa shops. The three-car *Blue Bird* operated a daily roundtrip between Minneapolis and Rochester, Minnesota, home of the world-famous Mayo Clinic.

The *Blue Bird* consisted of a Power/Railway Post Office (RPO)/Express car containing a Winton 300 horsepower V-6 engine; a 74-seat coach; and a parlor-club-observation. The parlor-club-observation included two Pullman sections reserved for Mayo Clinic patients. Like many of its non-streamlined gas-car siblings, the *Blue Bird* operated into the 1930's.

The combination of diesel-electric power and stainless steel construction would herald the introduction of true stream-line railcar design.

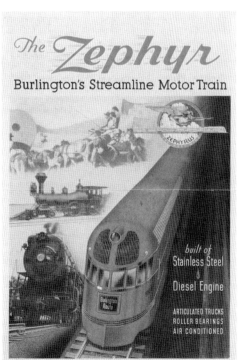

Cover of the pamphlet *The Zephyr, Burlington's Streamline Motor Train.*

Chapter 1

— The Great Depression —
Necessitates New Opportunity

As the country spiraled down into the Great Depression after the Wall Street crash of October 1929, General Motors' Vice President of Research was in the midst of his latest project. Charles F. "Boss Ket" Kettering was an inventive genius of near Thomas Edison stature, having developed numerous automotive, chemical and industrial products over the prior two decades. Items included the electric self-starter system, leaded "high test" gasoline, Duco and Dulux brand fast-drying enamels and lacquers, plus numerous other advanced products.

Olive K *Owner, Charles F. Kettering*

Designers - Cox and Stevens, Inc.
and John H. Wells, Inc.
Builders Defoe Boat and Motor Works
Length overall - - - - - 170 feet
Length waterline - - - - - 160 feet
Beam - - - - - - 26 feet
Draft - - - - - 9 feet, 6 inches
Machinery—Two Model 158-6, six-cylinder,
New-type, airless injection
Winton Diesel Engines — 500
H. P. each.

Charles Kettering's yacht *Olive K* equipped with two Winton 500 hp engines was 170 feet overall. *Bernard Golias collection*

tillate fuel was defined as anything the refinery didn't want or couldn't use after "cracking off" gasoline from the crude oil. It covered the range from low-grade gasoline to naphtha and kerosene.

Getting these fuels to burn in a beefed up gasoline engine was difficult. The engines required several carburetors—sometimes one per cylinder pair—and up to four spark-plugs per cylinder. Still, the need for higher horsepower existed, and at $0.03 per gallon vs. $0.15 for gasoline the cost incentive to continue development intensified as the Depression deepened.

Kettering believed he could develop a high speed diesel engine with a power-to-weight ratio of about 20 pounds per horsepower. He also believed a two-stroke cycle design was the way to proceed, with each downward stroke of the piston a power stroke. Such an engine would allow GM to expand into the railroad, bus, truck and heavy equipment markets.

Kettering purchased a yacht powered with Winton diesel engines in the spring of 1928 and returned to purchase a second, larger one using diesel-electric power in September of 1929. The twin 500 hp diesel engines in this yacht used Winton's new and patent-applied-for "unit injector" system to inject fuel into the cylinders. Each cylinder had its own injector. That eliminated the use of a single high-pressure fuel pump, connecting lines, and the attendant risk of fuel leakage and fire.

Kettering was so impressed with Winton and the unit injector concept that he recommended General Motors purchase the Winton Engine Company. They did so on June 20, 1930. Winton's largest customer, EMC, subsequently joined GM as a subsidiary corporation on December 31, 1930.

During the mid-1930's Winton Engine and Electro-Motive started development of a so-called distillate engine. Dis-

V-12 Engine Offered

In 1931 Winton introduced a 600 hp V-12 distillate engine followed by a whopping 900 hp V-12 in 1932. The 600 hp engine was reasonably successful, powering the last of the gas-electric cars and America's first streamline train—Union Pacific's M-10000—orders all received by EMC between 1931-33.

Only two of the 900 hp distillate engines were constructed, with one installed in Santa Fe motorcar M-190, the largest and most powerful ever built, which consisted of a power car containing the engine and controls articulated to a coach section. Although its 900 hp distillate engine was an evolutionary dead end, the use of articulation and truck-mounted brake cylinders would reappear in the design of the Zephyr.

For America's railroads in 1933 distillate and gasoline fuels belonged to the past. Diesel would be the power of the future.

From September 1930 through the end of 1932 development of a two-stroke cycle diesel prime mover progressed concurrently at the Winton plant in Cleveland and the GM Development Laboratory in Detroit. From single cylinder test units to in-line multiple-cylinder engines, once one problem was eliminated another would take its place.

Just some of the seemingly innumerable problems included providing constant pressure intake air flow and eliminating or minimizing main and connecting rod bearing failures, fuel injector clogging, seized piston rings and/or cracked pistons. All took their toll. Finally, by late 1932 six-cylinder engines producing about 80 hp per cylinder were performing reasonably successfully on test stands at Detroit and Cleveland.

Shotwelding Stainless Steel

While the internal combustion technicians were spending long, frustrating hours in Detroit and Cleveland, the ability to work and weld stainless steel was being developed in North Philadelphia, Pennsylvania.

In 1912 Krupp Steel of Germany developed stainless steel by adding 18% chromium and 8% nickel to regular carbon steel. This formed a much harder and corrosion-resistant metal soon known in the trade as stainless steel due to its gleaming, rustproof finish. Exceptionally malleable, it could be easily rolled into thin sheets containing great strength, particularly when those sheets were formed into rigid shapes by rolling, stamping or die drawing.

However, the new metal could not be welded by conventional means, and was so tough that drilling or punching the holes for rivets was prohibitively difficult. Thus stainless steel had few applications outside of the kitchen and medical field.

One man intrigued nearly to the point of obsession by the potential of stainless steel was Edward G. Budd of Philadelphia. Born in 1870, as a talented and aggressive young man he first learned the trade of machinist and subsequently rose to become general manager at the Hale & Kilburn Company, a Philadelphia-based manufacturer of railroad passenger car seats.

A confident individualist, Edward Budd struck out on his own in 1912, forming the E. G. Budd Manufacturing Company to supply preformed sheet steel stampings to the burgeoning automobile industry. Budd's small firm quickly rose to prominence as a supplier of various metal shaping and stamping equipment and complete subassemblies to the auto industry, including the welded steel wheel rim—still produced and in use today.

In 1929 Budd's chief engineer, a WWI Army Colonel named Earl J. W. Ragsdale, began intensive experimentation aimed at developing a process capable of welding stainless steel. By 1931 Colonel Ragsdale had developed just such a process that Budd patented and trademarked as Shotwelding. Heavy electrodes were placed on each side of the two stainless steel sheets to be joined. A low voltage, high amperage electric current carefully controlled between 1-and-20/120th of a second in length was then passed between the electrodes. This "shot" of electricity raised the temperature of the inner facing surfaces of the metal under the electrodes to between 2,600 and 2,700 degrees Fahrenheit, instantaneously melting and joining the sheets. Since the molten metal did not extend to the electrodes themselves, it was not exposed to or contaminated by atmospheric oxygen. A proper Shotweld melted between 50% and 80% of the metal contained between the two electrodes—but not out to the surface of the stainless steel touching either electrode—and resulted in a weld stronger than the adjacent metal.

Experiments With Shotwelding

Budd promptly began experimenting with this new process. Budd designed and Shotwelded together both a bus and plane in 1931, followed by several one- and two-car self-propelled rail passenger cars in 1932 and 1933. None were commercially viable, albeit their most successful component was undoubtedly their stainless steel frames and bodies.

All the components required to create the Zephyr were now at hand. Momentarily, Ralph Budd will enter the picture, and like a symphony orchestra conductor, make the whole greater than the sum of its parts.

The Winton 2-cycle 8-cylinder diesel engines, the type used by the famous Pioneer Zephyr, were the future of diesel locomotive power in the United States. These engines were on display in 1933-34 at the Century of Progress Exposition in Chicago, where they furnished power for the General Motors building. It was here that Ralph Budd, Burlington's president, saw the engines for the first time. *Bernard Golias collection*

Chapter 2

— A Season of Tribulation Brings New Hope —
The Zephyr Conceived

On December 8, 1931 Ralph Budd was elected to the presidency of the Chicago, Burlington & Quincy Railroad.

Strongest of the so-called granger lines, the CB&Q's main lines stretched from Chicago to Minneapolis/St. Paul, Chicago to Denver, and Denver to Galveston, Texas. Other main lines reached to St. Louis, Kansas City and Billings, Montana. "Everywhere West" was its slogan, and the "Q" covered America's heartland from the Mississippi River to the east slope of the Rocky Mountains.

The mild mannered, bespectacled Budd was well prepared for the office of CB&Q president. Born in 1879, he held a Civil Engineering degree from Highland Park College in Des Moines, Iowa, earned before his 20th birthday. In 1906 John F. Stevens, chief engineer overseeing construction of the Panama Canal, called Budd to come to Panama and manage construction of the Panama Railroad across the isthmus. Budd did. He was 27 years of age.

Ralph Budd joined the Great Northern Railroad in 1912, became its executive vice president in 1917 and its president two years later. Since Great Northern and Northern Pacific jointly owned and controlled the CB&Q, Ralph Budd also sat on the CB&Q's Board of Directors.

While chief executive of the Great Northern, Ralph Budd guided the 7.79-mile-long Cascade Tunnel—North America's longest—to completion on January 12, 1929 after only 38 months of construction. Diesel-powered electric generator sets had been employed to supply power at the Cascade Tunnel project. Budd noted how powerful, efficient and reliable the diesel-generator sets were. Budd also oversaw the June 10, 1929 inauguration of GN's new premier passenger service, the *Empire Builder*.

Budd Becomes President

Ralph Budd became CB&Q president on January 1, 1932. His sense of commitment and penchant for working 16 hour days was a given, otherwise he wouldn't have accepted the challenges which awaited him in the corner office that cold and bleak January morning.

By January of 1932 the Great Depression had gripped America and the world for more than two years. Industrial production was half or less what it had been in 1928 or 1929, and upwards of 25% of America's workers were unemployed. Even more were what today is referred to as underemployed.

The Burlington had carried 18 million passengers in 1924, and before the Depression hit in full force, the count was down to 13.8 million in 1929. The bottom was yet to be reached in 1932—that would be but 7 million tickets the following year. Revenue, too, was on the skids, sliding from a respectable $28.5 million in 1923 to only $6.7 million in 1933. The Burlington's operating income in January 1932 was a staggering 72% below that of January 1931. The problem sat squarely in Ralph Budd's lap, and it was his responsibility to deal quickly with it before the "Q" collapsed in bankruptcy.

One of the many ideas occupying Ralph Budd's mind during his first months in office was how to entice passengers back to Burlington Route trains. About 25% of the road's passenger service was handled plainly but efficiently by gas-electric car service. Another 25% was served by steam-powered 2-5 car local or accommodation trains where as Budd remarked, "Some trains had to be operated, but earnings were insufficient for any profit."

Fast and Flashy Train

Budd began mulling over how best to create a small, fast and flashy train that would be inexpensive to operate, eye catching and require minimal crew and maintenance. It would have to handle 70-80 passengers, 20-25 tons of freight and baggage, include a Railway Post Office compartment, and be internal combustion-powered.

In the early fall of 1932 Ralph Budd journeyed to Philadelphia and the offices of The Edward G. Budd Manufacturing Company. There, on September 29 he took a ride on the Budd Company's latest product, a stainless steel self-propelled rail car. It used a gasoline engine for propulsion and had pneumatic tires supplied by the Michelin Company of France via their US representative, Goodyear Tire, surrounded by steel flanged rings.

Ralph Budd questioned whether the gasoline engine and pneumatic tires would stand up under the rigors of daily railroad service, but that Shotwelded stainless steel frame was another matter. Stainless steel was several times stronger than carbon steel, while its exterior surface was a rustproof bright silver-gray that required no painting. The carbody had been Shotwelded together quickly and in a streamlined fashion without any visible rivet heads or buttwelded steel plate joints. The reduced maintenance and lighter weight a stainless steel car offered would quickly compensate for the stainless steel's higher initial cost and Shotweld fabrication. Any additional passenger or advertising "eye appeal" coming from the sparkling exterior finish was just so much added frosting on the cake!

When Budd returned from his Philadelphia visit he remarked to his Vice President Ed Flynn: "I've seen a thing that convinced me that stainless steel offered, at last, a means

This is an artist's rendering of early Budd Company 1930s trains: (top) Texas & Pacific's 1933 gasoline-powered two-car stainless steel train, mounted on rubber tires, was a forerunner of the T&Ps Eagle trains; (middle) the 1932 "Green Goose" single-car prototype gasoline-powered train; (foreground) the 1934 stainless steel #9900 Pioneer Zephyr.

of translating certain ideas concerning railway transportation into actuality."

Quest For New Concepts

In his quest for new concepts to incorporate in his envisioned streamliner, Budd later that fall of 1932—and perhaps on his way back to CB&Q headquarters in Chicago from Philadelphia—stopped to see Harold Hamilton at Electro-Motive in Cleveland. The "Q" was a good customer of EMC, having begun purchasing their gas-electric cars in 1927. The majority of the "Q's" 55-unit gas-electric car roster had been built by EMC/Winton and were the most efficient—but certainly not the most glamorous—pieces of passenger equipment on the railroad.

Harold Hamilton took Ralph Budd to Winton Engine and showed him the progress on the two-stroke cycle diesel prototypes. Wanting to learn more, Budd was directed by Hamilton and Winton President George Codrington to Charles Kettering at GM in Detroit. When Budd arrived at the GM Research Laboratory in December 1932, Kettering showed him the new in-line 6-cylinder Model 201 prototype cranking away on a test stand. Ralph Budd took a long look and flatly announced this was the engine to power his train of the future.

Taken aback at the chief executive's overt enthusiasm, Kettering responded: "Not yet. We wouldn't dare sell you this thing. We don't even know if it will run. General Motors has decided to give these prototypes a test run powering our Chevrolet Exhibit at the Century of Progress Exhibition in Chicago this summer. Go take a look at them and see what you think."

It was a meeting Ralph Budd anticipated with great enthusiasm.

By mid-winter 1932-33 his new train concept was complete. It would be streamlined; framed and sheathed in Shotwelded stainless steel; several cars in length; moderne in interior appointment and color schemes; and diesel-electric powered. Nobody had seen the likes of it before, although competitor Union Pacific under W. Averill Harriman in conjunction with Pullman was supposedly planning to build a small distillate-powered aluminum streamliner of its own.

Time would tell.

The Pioneer Zephyr sits in front of the Edward G. Budd Manufacturing Co. plant in Philadelphia in April of 1934, awaiting more work, including installation of the Burlington Route shield below the front windows.

Chapter 3

— 1933: Conception and Construction —

The spring of 1933 was the turning point of the Great Depression. Bread lines, soup kitchens and "Hooverville" shanty towns were still plentiful, but a new optimism was slowly beginning to seep across America.

Newly-elected President Franklin D. Roosevelt had thundered, "We have nothing to fear (fea-ah) but fear itself" from the Capitol steps in his inauguration address of March 4, 1933, and his controversial New Deal legislation was taking innovative steps in the minds of a majority of Americans to ameliorate and hopefully reverse the economic collapse afflicting America.

Chicago's A Century of Progress Exposition—the ultimate expression of American self help and optimistic thinking in that grim year—was designed to promote the face of a wonderful, prosperous and generally better and more advanced tomorrow. Accordingly, Ralph Budd had signed up for an exhibition track to show off the public face of the Burlington Route in the best possible light.

On a short exhibition track the "Q" exhibited new (1930) Baldwin-built 4-6-4 Hudson type steam locomotive #3000 with a six-car heavyweight train consisting of a Railway Post Office car, a coach or chair car, two Pullmans of differing layouts, a diner and a lounge car. A train of greater length but a similar consist, the *Aristocrat*, daily connected Chicago with Denver. The 1,034-mile run was scheduled for 25 hours and 45 minutes.

Credibility on the Line

Also present at the Exposition was the General Motors pavilion which contained a miniature Chevrolet assembly line powered by two Winton Model 201A in-line 8-cylinder diesel engines directly connected to General Electric DC generators. Barely completed in time for the Exposition's opening with little or no time for testing, the diesel-electric power plants stood completely surrounded by glass walls, in the public eye for the first time, and GM's credibility was on the line for all to see.

Although much had been accomplished in the GM Research Laboratory in Detroit and at Winton Engine in Cleveland over the winter of 1932-33, those two Winton diesel engines on the shore of Lake Michigan were little more than prototypes. Nearly two decades later their mentor, Eugene Kettering, son of "Boss Ket" and employed at Winton Engine in Cleveland on the two-stroke cycle diesel engine project, recalled the engines' installation and operation with a telling commentary: "...The flow of rush parts from Cleveland and Detroit to Chicago was fearful and wonderful. The boys worked all night and hoped the engines would run all the next day....

To mention the parts with which we had trouble in Chicago would take far too much time. Let it suffice it to say that I do not remember any trouble with the dip stick!"

Although Gene Kettering and his staff were growing ulcers and premature gray hair in Chicago, it was beside those yammering two-stroke cycle engines where Charles Kettering of GM, Harold Hamilton and his chief engineer—Richard Dilworth—of EMC, and Ralph Budd and his Assistant to the Vice President Fred Gurley met one late May or early June day in 1933.

'She Has Hopes'

Hamilton's appraisal was cautious and businesslike: "...You can only expect about 80,000 miles of cylinder life in these first Diesels.... However, I believe we can get an engine built for you soon enough not to delay the completion of your train." Dilworth, famous for his blunt speech, was more succinct: "She ain't much now. But she has hopes!"

By the end of the meeting a "very nervy railroad president" as Charles Kettering bluntly referred to Ralph Budd in subsequent correspondence, had his commitment from General Motors to supply two Winton Model 201A 8-cylinder diesel prime movers for his new train. The second engine was a spare.

Ralph Budd took a more sanguine position on the use of prototype General Motors' diesel power: "I knew that if General Motors was willing to put the [Winton 201A] engine in a train, the national spotlight would be on the Corporation. They'd simply have to stay with it until it was satisfactory. I knew they'd make good. Actually, I wasn't taking a chance at all."

Later that day in his office, Ralph Budd chaired an executive staff meeting that included Executive Vice President Fred Flynn, Assistant to the Vice President Fred Gurley and Passenger Traffic Manager Albert Cotsworth, Jr. Their new train needed a new name. Since it was, after all, the "latest word in transportation" one of the group decided to look up the literal last word in the English Dictionary. "Zymurgy" related to the process of fermentation was duly located—and promptly discarded.

God of West Wind

As the discussion continued, Ralph Budd recalled his recent rereading of Chaucer's Canterbury Tales, in which the God of the West Wind, Zephyrus, symbolized rebirth and renaissance. *That was it.* The new train would become the Zephyr. The Burlington Zephyr.

ABOVE. The power car of the Pioneer Zephyr sits in front of the Budd Company plant in Philadelphia as the unit nears completion. BELOW. The power car being constructed at the Budd plant; in cross section the car assumed somewhat of a tubular shape. *Bombardier, Don Heimburger collection*

From 14th Century English literature to 20th Century technology, Ralph Budd proved himself a Renaissance man. On June 17, 1933 the Chicago, Burlington & Quincy Railroad placed AFE (Authorization for Expenditure) #28022 with the Edward G. Budd Manufacturing Company of Philadelphia for "one streamline lightweight diesel-electric powered passenger train." Although the contract was with the Budd Company, it included specific subcontract provisions to GM subsidiaries Winton Engine Corporation for one two-stroke cycle diesel engine; Electro-Motive Corporation for the design and installation of the Winton engine along with a General Electric DC generator, traction motors, and electrical control equipment package; and Hyatt to supply roller bearings for all axles.

Air brakes and controls were to be supplied by Westinghouse. Interior design was to be done by Paul Phillipe Cret, noted interior designer and Dean of the University of Pennsylvania's School of Architecture, with assistance from the Chicago architectural design firm of Holabird & Root. The Massachusetts Institute of Technology was retained to do streamline "airflow" design tests in the wind tunnel on their Cambridge, Massachusetts campus.

Ralph Budd penned the announcement thus in a Foreword published in the April 14, 1934 issue of Railway Age magazine leading an article introducing the Zephyr and describing it in minute technical detail:

Only twenty per cent as much local traffic by rail was performed in 1933 as in 1920..... In departing from convention and undertaking to make improvements that would result in lower train operating costs with added travel comfort, our idea has been to call upon the industry which has taken from us much of our traffic, namely, the automobile industry.

We have accordingly collaborated with the Edward G. Budd Manufacturing Company, the General Motors Corporation and the Massachusetts Institute of Technology, and with two architectural firms, Paul Cret and Holabird & Root. These concerns were given carte blanche in designing and decorating the Zephyr without any restriction except those which are inherent to railway equipment, namely the gage of the track and the clearances within which the outside dimension must be kept.

The railways are very jealous of their record of safety, and stress was laid in our instructions that no compromise be made with safety but that insofar as possible the safety factors must be increased.

In the consideration of material, the character of which must provide the greatest strength with a minimum of weight, it was of paramount importance that we select a material not only uniform in structure, but one entirely non-corrosive (over) the entire service life of the train.

TOP. The observation car of the Pioneer Zephyr was called a solarium-lounge with seating for 12; the entrance is at the rear of the main passenger compartment. BELOW. The Zephyr was a complete departure from conventional design, with the entire body structure from floor to roof performing load-carrying functions. Main members of the car bodies were sideframes of a modified Pratt truss design which were carried up to the roof by the use of diagonals in wide deadlights between the windows, while the roof formed the top chord. *Bombardier, Don Heimburger collection*

TOP. This is a view of the Pioneer Zephyr looking into the engine room with the hatch and radiators removed. Note the two large fans at right and left front. MIDDLE. This is the exterior of the baggage and express compartment. The Pioneer Zephyr ran between Kansas City and Lincoln, Nebraska. BELOW. Trucks on the Zephyr were outside bearing type with cast-steel frames and bolsters. The wheels were 30" in diameter, although the power trucks featured 36" diameter wheelsets.

Although Budd claimed to have given carte blanche to his contractors in the design and fabrication of the new Zephyr, in reality he left little to chance as to what Budd, GM and associates were expected to deliver.

The Order Placed

At the "Q" Board of Directors meeting on July 11, 1933 Budd stated:

(An) order has been placed for a Diesel-driven stainless-steel train capable of traveling at a speed of 120 miles per hour. The train will comprise three cars built as an articulated unit along aerodynamic lines, will weigh about 169,000 pounds (84.5 tons) and have a total seating capacity of 70. The first car will contain the motor, baggage and mail compartment; second car, baggage and express, with a buffet and smoking compartment in the rear to seat 19 passengers; third car will be entirely devoted to seating space with a capacity of 51, which includes 12 parlor chairs. The overall length of the train will be approximately 196 feet, and the estimated cost $200,000.

It was a de facto refinement of his concept envisioned by early 1933. Burlington staff Mechanical Engineer C. E. Anderson relocated to Philadelphia within weeks of the contract signing in order to oversee the Zephyr's design and construction at the Budd factory. Likewise, John A. Holabird, principal of the interior design firm Holabird & Root, was a personal friend of Ralph Budd. Little occurred at Budd's Hunting Park plant or Paul Cret's Philadelphia design office that didn't filter back to the Burlington's Chicago headquarters over the next nine months.

Settle Down to Work

After the unrecorded but inevitable celebrations in Philadelphia, Cleveland and Detroit upon receipt of the signed order, the designers, draftsmen, and engineers settled down to work. What ultimately totaled a $208,561.88 order [including two extra GE traction motors and one extra Winton diesel engine] was largely split between Budd and General Motors' subsidiaries EMC and Winton Engine. A substantial sum in 1933, roughly equivalent to more than $4 million today, it also represented upwards of 80,000 man-hours of labor for employees of Budd, GM and their roughly 100 subcontractors or vendors. Christmas 1933 was merrier and the New Years of 1934 loomed brighter in many a household that would have otherwise been bleak and dreary without the Burlington Route's gamble on its new Zephyr.

The research and overall design of the Zephyr was the responsibility of Albert Dean, a recent Massachusetts Institute of Technology aeronautical engineering graduate on Budd's

INSET. The sleek, trim look of the Zephyr is apparent in this profile view of the lead car at the Budd plant. ABOVE. The Zephyr featured a continuous stainless-steel roof panel finished and Shotwelded into place. *Burlington Northern Santa Fe Railway* BELOW. The one-piece alloy welded engine bed featured increased strength and a reduction of weight. *Burlington Northern Santa Fe Railway*

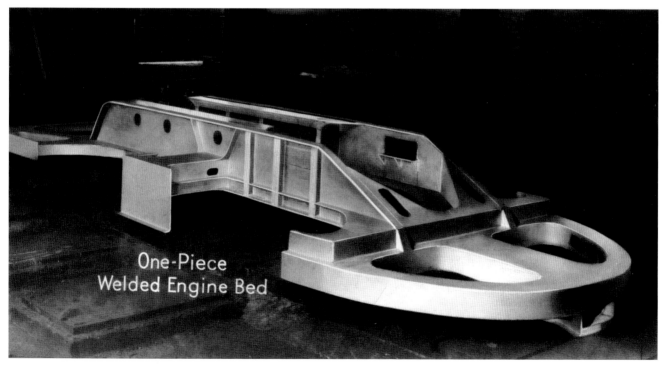

A Budd workman motions to a crane operater as a stainless steel Shotwelded Zephyr car is fabricated in the Budd Company shops. *Burlington Northern Santa Fe Railway*

ABOVE. Side view of the end car of the train which featured a writing desk with lamp at the rear centerpoint, writing tables both sides and ash trays secured to the floor. RIGHT. The Zephyr under construction in the Budd plant. The fluted paneling under the windows was clipped to the Shotwelded frame. *Bombardier, Don Heimburger collection*

payroll. His job was to craft the Zephyr's final exterior and load bearing design from raw engineering data and innumerable slide rule calculations. His brother, Walter, an MIT mechanical engineer, was responsible for the power plant and running gear design of the new train.

John Harberson, an associate in Paul Cret's firm, was a frequent visitor to the Budd plant, who provided updates to the interior design and decor.

Mockups Are Tested

Early summer of 1933 found various wooden Zephyr models and mockups being tested in the MIT wind tunnel at Cambridge, Massachusetts. The chosen design had 47% less drag—or wind resistance—than a steam-powered three-car conventional train at 95 miles per hour.

In an additional acknowledgment of aircraft design influence, the Zephyr's running and marker lights were airplane wing lights installed in Budd-built housings.

As summer turned to fall and then early winter, the shuffle of paper in the drafting and design areas was replaced by the sounds of metal being shaped and Shotwelded. Busy too, were the men at EMC, Winton, GE, Westinghouse, Hyatt and elsewhere as they fabricated, tested and prepared major components and subassemblies for shipment.

MOTOR-MAIL-BAGGAGE
CONTINUOUS RATING SPEED-40 M.P.H.
MAX. SPEED-117 M.P.H
LENGTH-71'-11 5/8"-74'-6 1/8" OVER PILOT.
GEAR RATIO-52:25

BAGGAGE

KIT.-DINETTE-COACH
8 SEATS-DINETTE
32 PASS.-COACH

COACH-PARLOR
40 PASSENGER-COACH
12 " -PARLOR
52 " -TOTAL

TRAIN NO.9900	NAME-PIONEER	CAR NO.	505	500	570
HORSEPOWER	600	TYPE CAR	BAGGAGE	DINETTE-COACH	COACH-PARLOR
TRAIN CAR NO.	1	2	3	4	
WEIGHT ON FRONT TRUCKS / WEIGHT ON REAR TRUCKS	PASSENGER CAPACITY	0	40 REV.	52 REV.	
92,300	WEIGHT OF CAR LIGHT-LBS. 52940	59,350	54,760	32130	
100,600	WEIGHT OF CAR READY TO RUN. LBS. 55,600	64,900	56,700	32500	
104,900	WEIGHT OF CAR NORMAL MAX. LOAD LBS. 80,830	82,250	62800	37250	
LENGTH OF CAR COUPLED 74'-6 1/8"	58'-8"	64'-0"	64'-0"		
AXLE SIZE #1X6"X11"	#2-6"X11" ARTIC.	#3-6"X11" ARTIC.	#4-5 1/2"X10" ARTIC.	#5-4 1/4"X8"	
FUEL OIL GALS. 600	COLOR SCHEME				
LUBRICATING OIL GALS. 80	BUILT BY- BUDD	BUDD	BUDD		
COOLING WATER GALS. 140	YEAR BUILT 1934	1938	1934		
HEATING BOILER-LBS./HR. 500	BUILDER FLOOR PLAN NO. BUDD SK-5840	BUDD SK:13799	BUDD SK.5840		
BOILER WATER-GALS. 250					
BUILDER FLOOR PLAN - BUDD SK.5840					
YEAR BUILT 1934					

PIONEER ZEPHYR
CONSIST SUMMARY

TRAIN CAR NO.	TYPE CAR	WEIGHT OF CAR-LBS.		PASSENGER CAPACITY	
		READY TO RUN	NORM.MAX.LOAD	REV.	NON-REV.
1	MOTOR-MAIL BAGGAGE	100,800	104,900	0	0
2	BAGGAGE	55,600	80,830	0	0
3	KITCHEN-DINETTE-COACH	64,900	82,250	40	0
4	COACH-PARLOR	56,700	62800	52	0
		32,500	37,250		
TOTAL		310,300	388030	92	0

TOTAL NORMAL MAXIMUM LOAD OF TRAIN = 368,030# = 768 LBS. PER H.P.

TOTAL WEIGHT OF TRAIN, READY TO RUN, = 310,300# = 647 LBS. PER H.P.

TOP. Because of limited passenger capacity, in June of 1935 the Burlington ordered a fourth chair car for the Zephyr. The train had cut $.24 a mile off operating and maintenance costs when compared with steam-powered trains. These are the folio drawings of the four-car train as configured between 1938 and 1950.

Ralph Budd was so enamored with stainless steel car construction that he arranged to have a two-car gas-electric built by Budd for the Texas & Pacific RR visit the "Q" on its way from Philadelphia to Texas in October of 1933. At least one test run of the car was made on the Burlington's triple track Chicago to Aurora main line as far west as the suburb of Berwyn, Illinois.

The lightweight stainless steel cars were stunning to view, glowing in bright sunlight, while the passenger compartment was moderne in its interior design and decoration. Ralph Budd's enthusiasm for the two-car pocket streamliner was limited to its stainless steel construction. He had well founded reservations about the use of gasoline engines and the Michelin pneumatic tire system. The car would subsequently justify his concerns by being a complete operational and mechanical failure on the Texas & Pacific.

By mid-January 1934 Budd had the stainless steel frames and side sheathing of all three cars nearing completion and none too soon, as major components began to arrive almost daily at Hunting Park for installation in one of the three gleaming car bodies.

Zephyr Completed

The Zephyr's three car sections were completed on April 4, 1934. Too tall to be removed from the Budd plant on their own trucks, over the next three days each individual section was placed on dollies and rolled outside where they were trucked and assembled into the complete train.

On April 7, 1934 the Zephyr posed for its official portrait

Texas & Pacific's two-car stainless steel train was introduced in 1933. The lead car contained the power plant, railway post office and baggage/express compartment. The second car accommodated 76 passengers in air-conditioned comfort. The train was out of service within a year thanks to its failure-prone pneumatic tire system. *Bombardier, Don Heimburger collection*

With the advent of the Pioneer Zephyr, the Burlington Railroad was eager to promote its new mode of transportation. This three-car model was built to embody the new Zephyr.

and awaited preliminary test runs. Proud father Ralph Budd posed in the cab with straw boater hat in hand. Ten husky men and a boy pulled the train a few feet to prove—at least in front of the publicity cameraman—just how lightweight and free-rolling the roller bearing-equipped streamliner was.

Posed under the large E. G. Budd Mfg. Co. sign with its shovelnose prominently displaying the Burlington Route herald, there was no doubt that the joint venture, as it were, of Messieurs Budd, Budd and Kettering was about to make a remarkable and industry changing entrance onto the railroad stage of 1934.

On April 9 the Zephyr warmed its Winton diesel engine and roller bearing journals on a test run over the Reading Railroad between Philadelphia and Perkiomen Jct., a one-

way distance of 24.8 miles. With Burlington Route Master Mechanic and Road Foreman of Engines Jack Ford at the throttle (and a Reading engineer or road foreman of engines behind him in the cramped cab), CB&Q #9900 hit 104 mph with smiles all around. The grins were tempered by the memory that EMC and Winton mechanics had struggled for four days the prior week before getting that Winton diesel engine to turn over and fire.

Although Ralph Budd and Edward Budd were unrelated to each other except in matters of business and vision, their combined efforts in public relations to introduce the Zephyr to a curious American public would be innovative, extensive and sometimes downright humorous.

Budd's Zephyr was now ready for the Big Time.

This is an early view produced by the Budd Company of the front of the Pioneer Zephyr. The top front headlight was a 14-inch, 250-watt Golden Glow unit; inset marker lamps were airplane wing lights in housings made by Budd. A distinguishing mark of the Pioneer Zephyr is its slightly irregular lines above the front windows. *Bombardier, Don Heimburger collection*

Chapter 4

— The Zephyr in Detail —

The modest train that stood outside The Edward G. Budd Manufacturing Company plant in North Philadelphia on the morning of April 9, 1934 was markedly different than any other passenger train in America.

From slanted shovelnose to gently boat-tailed rear observation lounge, all 197' 2" of its three gleaming fluted stainless steel cars bespoke the latest engineering technology, artistic and decorating sophistication, and speedy service with panache aplenty.

Steam, steel and velvet plush seats were instantly, dramatically and irrevocably *passé*.

A description of CB&Q #9900 begins with the Zephyr's rounded 23°—from the vertical—sloped shovelnose. The operator's cab was immediately behind the nose with the engineer, or motorman, and his assistant engineer, or "fireman," separated from each other by the main generator.

The DC generator was directly attached to the diesel prime mover located behind the cab. Next came a 30' railway post office compartment equipped with sorting racks, while a 19' storage-mail area filled the remainder of the 71' 5" power car. Both the RPO and storage-mail areas had hardwood maple flooring over cork soundproofed sub floor. The power car's maximum height was 12' 1³/16", and it had a center of gravity 50³/4" above the rails.

Middle Car

The middle car, #505, was 57' 8" long and consisted of a 30' checked baggage and express compartment also equipped with maple flooring. Next came the 5' 6" buffet-grill, a vestibule and a 16' long smoking (coach) section containing 20 leather-covered seats. The car's height was 11' 2 3/16", and it had a center of gravity only 52" above the rails.

The 63'6"-long tail car, #570, contained 40 mohair-covered coach seats separated by a vestibule and restrooms from the 12-seat parlor observation lounge at the rear. The car's height and center of gravity were the same as the middle car.

The gleaming Shotwelded stainless steel was the most visible difference between the Zephyr and all other trains nationwide.

Its only true contemporary, and America's first streamline train, was the Union Pacific's distillate-powered, 116 seat, M-10000, introduced on February 12, 1934, only two months earlier. However, the M-10000 was of riveted aluminum alloy, had a plain—but aluminum trimmed—interior, and although virtually as fast as the Zephyr at 109 mph, UP's Little Zip would last in service only until mid-December of 1941. Sold for aluminum scrap on February

13, 1942, the M-10000's most lasting legacy was the introduction of internal combustion combined with streamlined design and UP's yellow and brown (now gray) paint scheme.

However, the 208,061 lb. Zephyr (without passengers, provisions or fuel) was far from constructed of only stainless steel. Just the carbody frame, trusses, roof and exterior sheathing were of this new wonder metal.

The exceptional strength of the stainless steel carbody began with the use of a modified Pratt (type) truss design on the car sides to which the exterior Shotwelded side sheathing added strength. Additional strength and structural stability came from the lateral roof trusses being Shotwelded directly to the sideframes and reinforced by corrugated stainless steel roofing Shotwelded to the trusses.

The floor beams were Shotwelded to the walls and corrugated subflooring was Shotwelded to the floor beams. Ultimately, this Shotwelded so-called frameless construction formed a comparatively light, tube-like structure so rigid that no center I-beam was necessary, eliminating tons of weight.

'Belly Pan'

For aerodynamic benefit a rounded "belly pan" of fluted stainless steel formed a tubular bottom beneath each car's floor. It added no structural integrity to the carbody but did protect underbody-mounted equipment from flying ballast at high speed. To fabricate each individual carbody required about 120,000 of the 3/16" diameter Shotwelds.

The heaviest single component of the Zephyr was a solid 6,070 lb. weldment of Cromansil (chromium-manganese-silica) alloy steel. It formed the power car's combined frame, engine bed, front truck bolster, front sill, anticlimber and collision post. Weldments forming the articulated joints between the cars were also constructed of Cromansil steel.

Cromansil could not be Shotwelded, so the weldments were riveted to the stainless steel car frames. Corrosion would be found decades later in these dissimilar metal joints, one of the few places it could be found in the stainless steel-framed Zephyr.

Cromansil steel was developed and supplied by Luken Steel of Coatesville, Pennsylvania. A subsidiary, Lukenweld, Inc., developed a highly accurate arc welding process for heavy steel plate and fabricated all the Cromansil steel weldments used on the Zephyr. The Lukenweld process was also used by GM's Winton Engine Corporation to fabricate the welded steel block of the Model 201A diesel engine.

Including the weight of the steel trucks, power plant

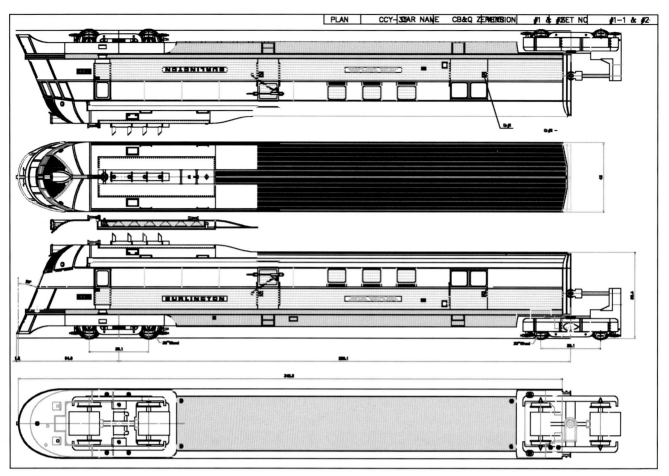

The Zephyr drawings on this and the following page are scale model plans for the June 1935 four-car Pioneer Zephyr provided by River Raisin Models for their scale model train. *Courtesy Jim Kindraka/Dan Navarre/River Raisin Models*

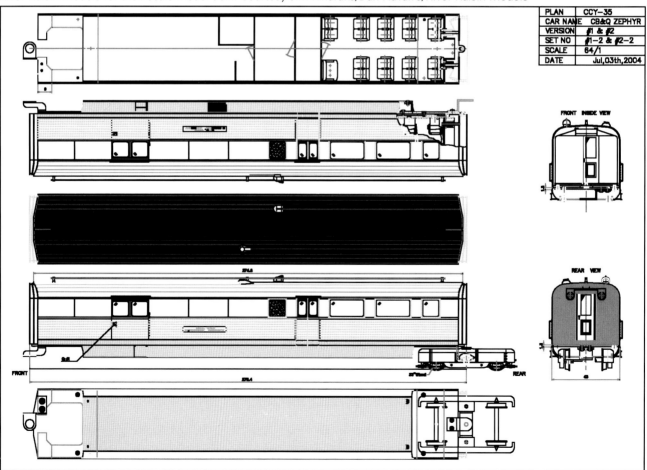

PLAN	CCY-35
CAR NAME	CB&Q ZEPHYR
VERSION	#1 & #2
SET NO	#1-2 & #2-2
SCALE	64/1
DATE	Jul,03th,2004

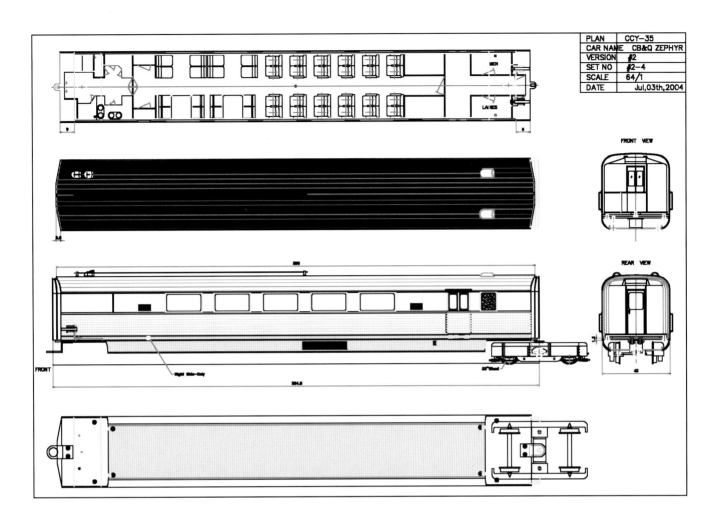

PLAN	CCY-35
CAR NAME	CB&Q ZEPHYR
VERSION	#2
SET NO	#2-4
SCALE	64/1
DATE	Jul, 03th, 2004

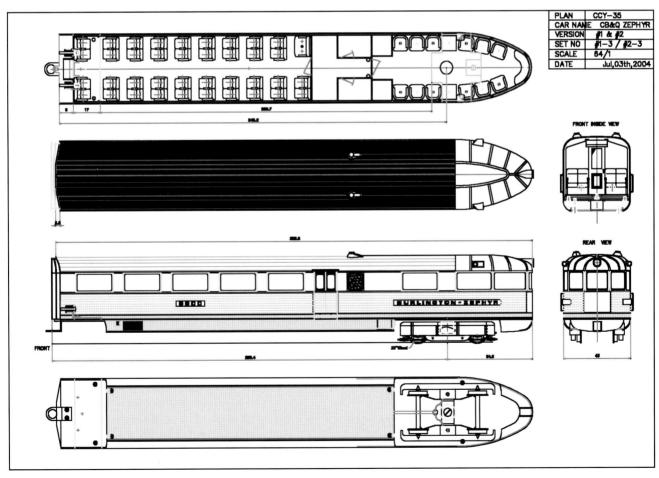

PLAN	CCY-35
CAR NAME	CB&Q ZEPHYR
VERSION	#1 & #2
SET NO	#1-3 / #2-3
SCALE	64/1
DATE	Jul, 03th, 2004

The full three-car Zephyr train is finished and sits beside the Budd Company plant in Philadelphia in 1934. Vestibule passages between the cars were enclosed by diaphragms bolted to the ends of the carbodies.

and the Cromansil frame components, more than 50% of the gross weight of the Zephyr was non-stainless steel.

The Zephyr rode on four roller bearing-equipped sprung equalized trucks. The power truck utilized 36" wheels, while the other three trucks used 30" wheels. At 90 mph the non-powered wheelsets rotated at 1,000 rpm!

The Zephyr was articulated; that is, the ends of adjacent carbody sections sat atop a shared single truck. The center car was designed so that it could be jacked up off its articulated connections at each end, allowing the front and rear cars to remain trucked for easy moving. Apparently this was done on the presumption that the power car and main passenger car would require the most frequent service, while the middle car with the baggage/express section and buffet would need less frequent attention.

Fourth Car Added

However, as valid as this presumption was in April of 1934, it was rendered moot when the fourth car was added to the train in June of 1935. Of course, that carbody had to have one upper and one lower articulated connection!

The walls and roof of the Zephyr were insulated with "Alfol," multiple layers of very thin aluminum foil crinkled together, which was very lightweight and fireproof. Flat panels between the windows, known as "deadlights," were constructed of plywood overlaid with stainless steel sheet.

The front truck carried two traction motors and bore the majority of the weight of the diesel engine, generator and their Cromansil engine bed and mounting frame, some 97,103 lbs. The second truck carried the combined weight of the rear end of the first car, and the front of the second, for a total of 50,249 lbs. An identical arrangement was used between cars two and three and carried 43,825 lbs., while the truck under the observation car carried only 27, 640 lb.

The articulated design, lower center of gravity, and decreasing weight toward the rear of the train allowed the Zephyr to snake gracefully through curves at higher speeds than conventional equipment. However, articulated equipment came with a hefty operational price. Any problem with any car in the set took the entire equipment set or train itself out of service. The Burlington Route would order no more articulated equipment after the delivery of the two 6-car Twin Zephyr sets in November of 1936.

Power for the Zephyr came from an in-line 8-cylinder Winton two-stroke cycle diesel engine with an 8" bore and 10" stroke. The engine was rated 660 *gross* horsepower at

The Pioneer Zephyr took the place of two locomotives and six cars having a total weight of 1.6 million pounds, or more than eight times the weight of the new Zephyr. Here the new Zephyr is posed on the siding into the Budd plant in North Philadelphia.

This picture was shot as a publicity stunt by the Budd Company to show how lightweight the four-car Zephyr was. Ten men and a youngster pull the train on April 8, 1934 to show that it could be done.

750 RPM's, of which 600 hp was available for traction, the remaining 60 hp being auxiliary power for air conditioning, lights, fuel pump, air compressor and the like.

The diesel engine was attached by a flexible steel coupling disk to a General Electric direct current electric generator. The generator fed up to 750 volts of direct current to twin 300 horsepower traction motors located beside the axles in the front truck and geared directly to them. The generator protruded into the cab area itself, physically separating the motorman (as the Burlington initially referred to the engineer) from the fireman on the opposite side of the noisy, miniscule cab.

The advantages of the use of diesel-electric power and stainless steel might be of general interest to the traveling public, but when Mr. and Mrs. John Q. Public entered and sat down in the Zephyr, they instantly realized a new age of people pleasing rail travel was at hand.

Never before had they seen the likes of the smooth pastel rose painted walls accented with golden rose window drapes in the 20-seat smoking compartment. The aluminum frame seats were upholstered in medium brown leather, and the floor was covered with dark linoleum tile.

The 40-seat main passenger compartment was painted a warm gray with a hint of green. These coach seats were upholstered in mohair with a gray-green stripe on a gold background. Silk window drapes matched the green of the upholstery. A taupe-colored seamless carpet covered the floor.

The observation lounge had gray painted walls containing a purple-blue tint. The window drapes were gold, and

The Burlington Railroad made good use of the advent of the Pioneer Zephyr to promote its passenger trains, producing this booklet to attract more riders.

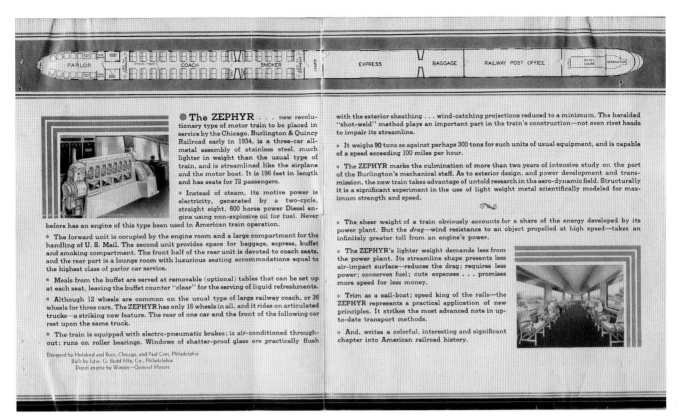

The ZEPHYR . . . new revolutionary type of motor train to be placed in service by the Chicago, Burlington & Quincy Railroad early in 1934, is a three-car all-metal assembly of stainless steel, much lighter in weight than the usual type of train, and is streamlined like the airplane and the motor boat. It is 196 feet in length and has seats for 72 passengers.

• Instead of steam, its motive power is electricity, generated by a two-cycle, straight eight, 600 horse power Diesel engine using non-explosive oil for fuel. Never before has an engine of this type been used in American train operation.

• The forward unit is occupied by the engine room and a large compartment for the handling of U. S. Mail. The second unit provides space for baggage, express, buffet and smoking compartment. The front half of the rear unit is devoted to coach seats, and the rear part is a lounge room with luxurious seating accommodations equal to the highest class of parlor car service.

• Meals from the buffet are served at removable (optional) tables that can be set up at each seat, leaving the buffet counter "clear" for the serving of liquid refreshments.

• Although 12 wheels are common on the usual type of large railway coach, or 36 wheels for three cars, The ZEPHYR has only 16 wheels in all, and it rides on articulated trucks—a striking new feature. The rear of one car and the front of the following car rest upon the same truck.

• The train is equipped with electro-pneumatic brakes; is air-conditioned throughout; runs on roller bearings. Windows of shatter-proof glass are practically flush

Designed by Holabird and Root, Chicago, and Paul Cret, Philadelphia
Built by Edw. G. Budd Mfg. Co., Philadelphia
Diesel engine by Winton—General Motors

with the exterior sheathing . . . wind-catching projections reduced to a minimum. The heralded "shot-weld" method plays an important part in the train's construction—not even rivet heads to impair its streamline.

• It weighs 90 tons as against perhaps 300 tons for such units of usual equipment, and is capable of a speed exceeding 100 miles per hour.

• The ZEPHYR marks the culmination of more than two years of intensive study on the part of the Burlington's mechanical staff. As to exterior design, and power development and transmission, the new train takes advantage of untold research in the aero-dynamic field. Structurally it is a significant experiment in the use of light weight metal scientifically modeled for maximum strength and speed.

• The sheer weight of a train obviously accounts for a share of the energy developed by its power plant. But the *drag*—wind resistance to an object propelled at high speed—takes an infinitely greater toll from an engine's power.

• The ZEPHYR's lighter weight demands less from the power plant. Its streamline shape presents less air-impact surface—reduces the drag; requires less power; conserves fuel; cuts expenses . . . promises more speed for less money.

• Trim as a sail-boat; speed king of the rails—the ZEPHYR represents a practical application of new principles. It strikes the most advanced note in up-to-date transport methods.

• And, writes a colorful, interesting and significant chapter into American railroad history.

These are the inside two pages to another 1934 Burlington Railroad 3⅓ x 6" foldout brochure which promoted "A Gleaming Shaft of Stainless Steel." *Don Heimburger collection*

the carpet was a platinum-gray. The lounge chairs had brushed aluminum frames and were upholstered in a purple-blue with gold background fabric. The Formica-covered side tables were finished in the same shade of blue as the upholstery, and had drop leaves with edges banded by aluminum accent stripes.

Smooth Masonite paneling covered all passenger compartment walls. Agasote millboard was used for the curved headlining and ceiling panels, all of which were painted light cream. Stainless steel accent strips ran the length of each compartment above the window line and along the open side of the recessed lighting strips. Lighting was indirect, and all windows had stainless steel sills.

The Zephyr as delivered had no fixed dining tables. Patrons could stand and eat at the small buffet counter, but generally the buffet attendant brought prepared meals to the passenger's seat. For serving meals to groups of two or four passengers in either the smoking or non-smoking coach sections, there were several small Formica-covered portable tables designed with one end that would clip into a wall bracket while the opposite end stood on a single folding leg. These tables were also convenient for card games and the like. First class passengers had the use of two side tables with drop down leaves in the parlor-observation lounge.

The aluminum-framed coach seats were supplied by the Hale & Kilburn Company, Edward Budd's former employer. Designed with 18" under seat clearance so passengers could store hand baggage, they were the direct predecessors to today's airliner seat with its carry on luggage location.

The seat design, at least in the non-smoking section, included locking anchors in each seat base so the legs of

portable trays, not dissimilar to the drop-down ones built into the backs of today's airliner seats could be attached. The buffet attendant first brought the tray, attached it to the base of the seat ahead, and then served the meal to the coach passenger. Trays of a similar design had arms that slid into locking slots on the front of each arm of the parlor chairs in the observation lounge.

These designs seemed to have materialized directly from the smartest supper clubs in New York, Chicago, or Los Angeles and in a sense, thanks to the skills of Paul Cret, John Haberson, John Holabird and associates, they had.

The train was equipped with a Stromberg-Carlson brand 11-tube radio with speakers behind decorative grills in each of the three passenger compartments as well as in the baggage compartment.

Heating was provided by steam from a 500-lb./hr oil-fired "flash" boiler from the Vapor Car Heating Company. Fin-type heaters were installed along the car sides at floor level, and heating coils were also installed in the ventilation and air conditioning duct system feeding each car. The 1.5-ton air conditioning system was supplied by York.

In sum, the Zephyr could carry 72 seated passengers in a bright, airy, comfortable, speedy and moderne-styled conveyance; feed them a modest breakfast, lunch and/or dinner; transport 25 tons of baggage and express; and do so in less than 200' of length, at the weight of about one and a quarter standard 85-ton Pullman sleeping car, and at 1/2-to-3/5th the cost of the steam-powered accommodation train it would replace.

A Depression-weary public was amazed and delighted, and their response was immediate and enthusiastic.

29

ABOVE. Edward J. Flynn, Burlington's operating vice president, and Edward G. Budd, president of the Budd Company, pose for the photographers in the Zephyr motorman's compartment. RIGHT. In front of America's first diesel-powered streamline train, Burlington Vice Presidents Edward Flynn and H. H. Holcomb pose with Edward Budd Sr. on April 8, 1934. BELOW. With the Zephyr still at the Budd plant, this photo was taken from inside the motorman's cab. The engine throttle is the long handle attached to the semi-circle bar at left.

Zephyr Makes World Record Run, 1017 Miles at Average of 78 an Hour

On Denver-Chicago Dash, Streamline Train Beats the Mark of Royal Scot, at Times Reaching 112 Miles an Hour— Cuts the Usual Running Time Nearly in Half.

Special to The New York Times.

CHICAGO, May 26.—Ushering in a new era in railroad transportation, the Burlington's streamline train, the Zephyr, arrived here from Denver tonight at the end of the longest and fastest non-stop run in railroad history.

Streaking over a distance of 1,015 miles between the Union Station in Denver and the Halsted Street Station in Chicago, the Diesel-motored silver tinted flier maintained an average speed of 77.6 miles an hour during its run of thirteen hours and five minutes.

The train cut twelve hours and forty minutes from the regular running time of the Aristocrat, the road's crack regular train.

The Zephyr left Denver at 7:04 (Central Daylight Time) this morning. Arriving at 8:09 o'clock tonight, the train negotiated the journey in one hour and fifty-five minutes better time than was expected by Burlington offi-

cials when the rail dash was planned. The goal aimed at was fifteen hours.

Half an hour after it had reached the Halsted Street Station the Zephyr moved onto the stage of the Wings of a Century, the transportation pageant at the World's Fair grounds.

In spanning a third of the continent the Zephyr's speed at times reached 112 1/2 miles an hour. The speed record of the nation on wheels is held by the Philadelphia & Reading—115.2 miles an hour over a 4.3 mile stretch between Brigantine Junction and Harbor, New Jersey.

Between Denver and Harvard, Neb., officials announced here, the train bettered by one hour and fifty-three minutes the 401-mile London-Glasgow record set by the Royal Scot in 1928. The Zephyr's time for the distance was five hours and four minutes. For this distance the Zephyr averaged 79.1 miles per hour as against

the Royal Scot's average of 56 miles an hour.

Passenger traffic along the entire route was sidetracked. Freight trains also were tied up. Switches were spiked to prevent tampering. At each station, where crowds were gathered to see the silver king of transportation speed through, the track was guarded by local law officers, posts of the American Legion and Boy Scouts.

Every road crossing over the 1,000-mile plus route was kept clear by a flagman. Difficult curves and isolated sections of trackage were watched by patrols of railroad men on foot and in motor cars. For days section gangs had worked on the tracks and road ballast, insuring that every spike and nut was in place for the supreme test of forward-looking railroading. Special placards warned the train's drivers as to practicable speeds along every part of the race course.

Railway Age magazine of April 14, 1934 published this photo of the Pioneer Zephyr, a week before the speedster train was introduced to the general public.

Engine Functions Perfectly

CHICAGO, May 26 (AP).—The 660-horsepower Diesel motor of the Burlington's Zephyr, which pushed the modernistic train along at record-breaking speeds in a non-stop dash from Denver to Chicago, functioned without a miss. Consistently the three-coach train, which weighs less than 100 tons, had accepted race challenges from airplanes and beaten them, officials of the road said.

Yet in its 1,015-mile journey averaging 77.75 miles an hour, the Zephyr sped for 96.3 miles at a sustained velocity of 90 miles, and reached a peak speed of 112 1/2 miles per hour, which it held for three miles, beating its own previous mark by three miles.

A crowd of about 100,000 at the World's Fair cheered enthusiastically tonight when, shortly after the Zephyr reached the Halsted Street station here, it wound its way over tracks in the city and appeared on Chicago's lake front.

The crowd covered the train's track with pennies to be mashed as souvenirs.

At the fair, the Zephyr was bunked in the Travel and Transport Building—representative of a new era of rail transportation and placed for exhibit beside an engine of the past—a Delaware & Hudson locomotive of 1827 vintage.

It was, said Ralph Budd, president of the Burlington, a great day in American rail history.

The trip, Mr. Budd said, demonstrated three things: "That the morale of the men and officers of the Burlington is proved by the way this run has been planned and carried out; second, the efficient condition of the railroad has been shown; third, the train performs fully up to expectations."

'Thrill' to Zephyr Pilot

Racing Train Didn't Give Crew a Minute's Worry, Says J. S. Ford.

By J. S. FORD, Assistant Master Mechanic, Burlington Railroad, Who Piloted the Zephyr Into Chicago.

(As told to the Associated Press.)

CHICAGO, May 26.—It was the thrill of a century for me to be at the controls of the Zephyr as it roared into Chicago at the completion of its record-setting run from Denver to Chicago.

There were three of us who shared the job of piloting the Burlington's ultra-modern speed train on the 1,015-mile trip. It was my good luck to be at the throttle for the last 165 miles. Our streamlined bullet certainly attracted the attention of the country.

I guess there were more than a million people who turned out along the route to see us go by. It seemed like the entire population was lined up at every town, city and village to cheer us along. Even the farmers in the fields got a big kick out of it.

Piloting that train was a wonderful sensation. It never gave us a minute's worry, and we burned up the rails. At times we reached a speed of 112 miles an hour, and they say we averaged seventy-seven miles an hour, although I haven't had time to figure it out yet.

Our wheels never stopped moving from the time we left Denver until we reached Chicago. The Zephyr held the road beautifully and responded to every touch. I'd like to do it again.

Start Delayed an Hour

Special to The New York Times.

DENVER, May 26.—The Burlington's streamlined train pulled out of the Union Station at 5:04 A. M. today (8:04 A. M. Eastern daylight saving time) on a new record-breaking non-stop run to Chicago.

The start was originally scheduled for 4 A. M. (Denver time), but a discovery of a faulty main bearing delayed the start. Mechanics made the discovery in a final inspection of the equipment at the Burlington shops late last night, finding that one of the roller bearings on the traction motor armature was damaged.

A replacement bearing was borrowed from the Union Pacific shops in Omaha and was brought here by plane, arriving shortly before midnight. Mechanics worked frantically to replace the damaged bearing, and for a while it looked as though the trip might have to be delayed even further.

C. J. Ince, general manager of the Western division of the Western Union,

was the official starter. He waved a flag and the train broke a tape attached to a clock which stopped at exactly 5:04:40 A. M., the clock hands bearing witness to the exact historic moment.

Aboard the Zephyr was a distinguished group of men who conceived and built this history-making train. The group included Ralph Budd, president of the Burlington and almost every high ranking official of that railroad. Edward T. Budd, president of the Budd Manufacturing Company of Philadelphia, which built the train, was on the train to watch the performance of his creation.

Seating Capacity Exceeded

H. L. Hamilton, president of the Winton Engine Company,* which developed the 660 horsepower Diesel motor of the train, also was a passenger.

In addition to large train crews, there was a staff of technical experts associated with companies who designed and built different parts of the train. There were more passengers than seats and extra chairs had to be placed in the express and baggage cars. Newspaper men comprised a large part of the passenger list.

The seating capacity of the train is seventy-two, but the passenger list exceeded eighty-five.

The Zephyr had a fuel supply of 600 gallons of crude ["furnace"] oil aboard. This is more than sufficient to make the run. The oil costs 4 cents a gallon and the total fuel bill for the Denver-to-Chicago run actually totalled only $17.

On the train also was Zeph, a Colorado burro, which was taken along as a mascot at the request of Ralph Budd. There was a last-minute rush here to obtain some hay for Zeph.

Hamilton was actually president of Electro-Motive Corp.

Interiors of the passenger compartments were finished in pleasing pastel shades with wall colors, window drapes, upholstery and floor coverings all contributing. The smoking compartment seats were upholstered in medium brown leather, and the floors covered with Linotile with a dark mottled surface that was neutral in tone.

Looking toward the rear of the Pioneer Zephyr, this April 1934 view shows the main coach seating arrangements. The car featured mohair-covered seats, indirect lighting, wall to wall carpeting and air conditioning.

Distance:
1015.4 miles (Denver Union Station to Halsted Street, Chicago) – speed run
+ 2.2 miles (Halsted Street to Travel and Transport Bldg., A Century of Progress World's Fair), 1934
Total 1017.6 miles

- Time (Denver to Halsted Street): 13 hours, 5 minutes, 4 seconds
- Left Denver at: 6:04:40 a.m. CST
- Arrived at Halsted Street (near 16th St.) in Chicago at 7:09:44 p.m. CST
- Arrived at Century of Progress World's Fair (near 31st St. and Lakefront) at 8:09:00 p.m. CST
- Weather along route: Generally fair, under high pressure, relatively cool (70s) no rain indicated anywhere along route

Known passengers and crew included:
Passengers
1. Ralph Budd, President, C.B.& Q. RR
2. Edward Flynn, Vice-President, C.B.& Q. RR
3. H.H. Holcomb, Vice-President, C.B.& Q. RR
4. Robert Rice, Vice-President, C.B.& Q. RR
5. T.J. Thomas, Asst. to President, C.B.& Q. RR
6. F.G. Gurley, Asst. to Vice-President, C.B.& Q. RR
7. W.E. Fuller, Asst. to Vice-President, C.B.& Q. RR
8. Albert Cotsworth, Passenger Traffic Manager, C.B.& Q. RR
9. A.W. Newton, Engineer, C.B.& Q. RR
10. H.H. Urbach, Supt. Motor Power, C.B.& Q. RR
11. Frank Darrow, Chief Engineer, C.B.& Q. RR
12. Neil Olsen, Special Agent, C.B.& Q. RR
13. Roy Baer, Mechanic, Electro-Motive Corp.
14. J.H. Aydelott, General Manager, Western Lines, C.B.& Q. RR
15. W.F. Thiehoff, General Manager, Eastern Lines, C.B.& Q. RR
16. E.C. Anderson, Mechanical Engineer, C.B.& Q. RR
17. Walter Anderson, son of E.C. Anderson
18. Thomas M. Henkle
19. H.H. Hamilton, President, Electro-Motive Corp.
20. Edward G. Budd, E. G. Budd Manufacturing Company
21. Hal Foust, Correspondent, Chicago Tribune
22. Garet Garret, Correspondent, Saturday Evening Post
23. Alan C. McIntosh, Correspondent, Lincoln Evening Journal-Star
24. Joseph McMeel, Correspondent, Rocky Mountain News (Denver)
25. Robert W. Rediske

Crew
1. Jack Ford, C.B.& Q. RR Assistant Master Mechanic (Engineer)
2. Ernie Weber, C.B.& Q. RR Superintendent of Automotive Equipment (Engineer)
3. Ernie Kuehn, Field Engineer, Electro-Motive Corp. (Engineer)
4. H.R. Clarke, C.B.& Q. RR (Pilot)
5. Harry C. Murphy, C.B.& Q. RR (Pilot)*
6. E.H. Piper, C.B.& Q. RR (Pilot)
7. W.O. Frame, C.B.& Q. RR (Pilot)
8. W.H. Dungan, C.B.& Q. RR (Road Foreman)
9. O.E. Hoenshell, C.B.& Q. RR (Road Foreman)
10. W.A. Stauss, C.B.& Q. RR (Road Foreman)
11. E. Milar, C.B.& Q. RR (Road Foreman)
12. Ray Wells, Conductor, C.B.& Q. RR
13. Ed J. Ross, Dining Car Inspector, C.B.& Q. RR
14. Wayne Wigton (Radio man)

Harry C. Murphy succeeded Ralph Budd as C.B.& Q. president in 1949 and served until 1965.

Fuel mileage:

- 600 gallons of diesel fuel ("furnace oil") carried

- 418 gallons of diesel fuel used (2.43 miles per gallon) @ 4¢/gallon
  Total cost: $16.72

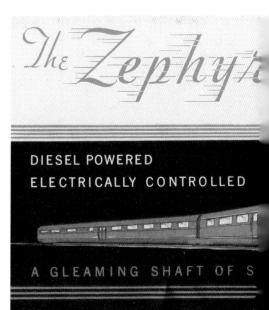

Scheduled railroad crews included the following:

	Motorman	Pilot	Road Foreman
Denver-Akron CO	E.F. Weber	H.R. Clarke	W.H. Dungan
Akron-McCook NE	J.S. Ford	H.C. Murphy	W.H. Dungan
McCook-Hastings NE	E. Kuehn	E.H. Piper	W.H. Dungan
Hastings-Lincoln NE	E.F. Weber	H.R. Clarke	O.E. Hoenshell
Lincoln-Creston IA	J.S. Ford	H.C. Murphy	W.A. Stauss O.E. Hoenshell
Creston-Ottumwa IA	E. Kuehn	W.O. Frame	W.A. Stauss
Ottumwa-Galesburg IL	E.F. Weber	H.R. Clarke	W.A. Stauss
Galesburg-Chicago IL	J.S. Ford	H.C. Murphy	E. Milar

Records considered significant in 1934:

Previous	Set by Zephyr
Distance Run at Top Speed	
Royal Scot	Zephyr
London-Edinburgh	Denver-Harvard (NE)
401 miles	401 miles
56 mph average	79.1 mph average
1928	1934
Highest Speed	
Philadelphia & Reading RR	Zephyr
Brigantine Junction (NJ)-Egg Harbor (NJ)	Yuma (CO)-Schramm (CO)
115.20 mph	112.50 mph
(4.5 miles)	(3 miles)

Burlington's New Motor Train

ESS STEEL

Christened the Burlington Zephyr on April 18, 1934 by Marguerite Cotsworth of Oak Park, Illinois, a Swarthmore College student, the Pioneer Zephyr then went on a five-week barnstorming tour of 25 Eastern cities. Marguerite was the daughter of Burlington Passenger Traffic Manager Albert Cotsworth, Jr. *Chris Burritt collection*

Chapter 5

— Tours, a Speed Record, the World's Fair — and Hollywood Stardom

The date of April 18, 1934 found CB&Q RR #9900 at the Pennsylvania Railroad's Broad Street Station in Philadelphia for its official introduction. The formal passing of ownership from the Budd Company to the CB&Q had occurred the day before as part of a press briefing "for the convenience of newspaper reporters, newspaper cameramen, and motion picture operators" before the train left its birthplace.

Prior to the ceremonies at Broad Street Station the Zephyr had two exhibition runs scheduled between 9 and 11 a.m., one to Paoli and a second to Downingtown.

At Broad Street Station wooden stanchions topped with clothesline held back the large, enthusiastic and fascinated crowd. Starting at 2:30 p.m. newsreel cameras rolled and a national audience listened via "the NBC chain broadcast," as Ralph Budd; Edward Budd; Alfred Sloan, president of General Motors; and William Irving, president of United States Steel, all made brief remarks. Similar laudatory comments followed from Pennsylvania Railroad President William W. Atterbury via radio connection from the NBC studio at Radio City, New York City, and from Gerard Swope, president of General Electric, via radio, as well.

'I CHRISTEN THEE...'

Then Miss Marguerite Cotsworth, an undergraduate at Swarthmore College in suburban Philadelphia and the daughter of Burlington Route Passenger Traffic Manager Albert Cotsworth, Jr., did the honors. With the words, "I christen thee Burlington Zephyr" she enthusiastically crashed a champagne bottle on the anticlimber surrounding the Zephyr's nose, and launched the God of the West Wind into railroad history.

At 4:00 p.m. the Zephyr departed Broad Street Station for Paoli and Downingtown, Pennsylvania trailing a steam-powered PRR train complete with camera crew taking movies of the Zephyr rolling down the multi-track main line slightly behind them.

Still photos taken at Broad Street Station and movie clips of the trip both clearly show an early type of antenna mounted on the roof of the Zephyr with signal leads going into the baggage room. Since NBC radio broadcast both the station ceremony and live from the train as it headed down the multiple track "Broad Way" to Downingtown, the antenna must have been part of the equipment used by NBC in its primitive live broadcast.

Trains were still deemed national news in 1934.

In early evening about 80 Pennsylvania, Burlington, Budd,

EMC/Winton managers, employees and invited guests boarded the Zephyr for a speedy 50-mile roundtrip jaunt to Paoli, Pennsylvania. The trip occurred between 8 and 9 p.m. that evening, and the three-car speedster attained 70-80 miles per hour upon several occasions.

Ralph Budd opined, "It looks like the beginning of a new era in transportation."

THREE WEEK TOUR

The next day the Zephyr was exhibited in Philadelphia at the beginning of a three-week-long tour of Northeast U.S. cities before heading west to Chicago and Burlington Route territory. More than 24,000 people visited the train in Philadelphia, and a whopping 109,000 people walked through the train on April 23-24, 1934 in New York City.

The introductory tour's climax was on May 10, 1934 when the westbound Zephyr averaged 80.2 miles per hour for 141 miles on the Pennsylvania Railroad between Fort Wayne, Indiana and the Chicago suburb of Englewood, Illinois against a constant headwind calculated at 39.8 mph. The Zephyr exceeded 100 mph numerous times during the 105-minute trip.

Between April 18 and May 23, when the Zephyr opened for display in Denver, Colorado, it visited 46 Midwest and Northeast cities and received 484,897 visitors! Streamline trains were fast gaining the attention of Americans from all walks of life.

Determined to capitalize on the publicity generated by the new Zephyr, Ralph Budd decided on a spectacular speed run to glean national attention for his new stainless steel speedster. The Zephyr would attempt a non-stop speed run from Denver to Chicago on Saturday May 26, 1934, taking about 13 hours to run the 1,015 miles from the "Mile High City" to the "Windy City." Once at Chicago it would continue down to the lakefront and officially open the second year of the 1933-34 Chicago Century of Progress Exposition.

For safety's sake crossing guards equipped with red flags would have to protect all 619 private road and 1,070 public highway crossings between Chicago and Denver. All track switches not in immediate use would be spiked closed in the main line position as well. Including Burlington RR employees, furloughed employees, local and railroad police, Boy Scouts, Kiwanis, and other volunteers, nearly 4,500 people guarded highway crossings on the Burlington between Denver and Chicago that memorable May 26, 1934.

The bold publicity gamble was nearly cancelled or postponed several times, and ultimately was accomplished only through great effort and selfless dedication of numerous em-

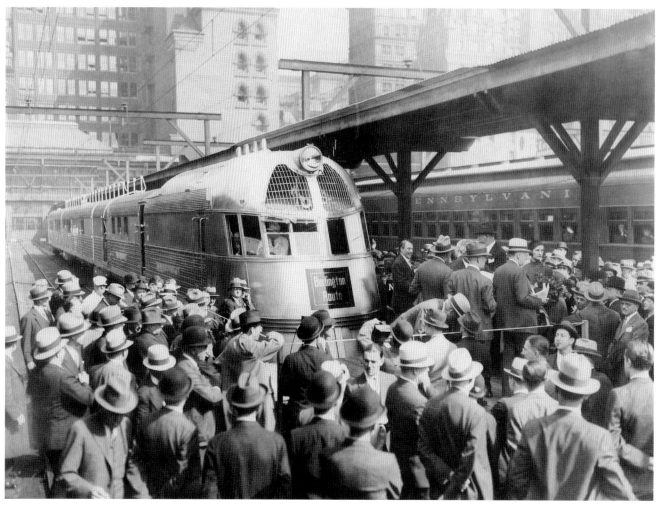

There was an exuberant crowd gathered for dedicatory services of the Pioneer Zephyr on April 18, 1934 at Philadelphia's Broad Street Station. The train had been officially turned over to the Burlington Railroad the previous day.

Ralph Budd, left, president of the Burlington Railroad; Carroll Burton, vice president, and G.C. Kimball, executive vice president, both of Carnegie-Illinois Steel Corp., inspect an O gauge "Flying Yankee" set masquerading as a miniature "Zephyr" at a National Railroad Appliances exhibit.
Fred G. Korth

Christening of Burlington Zephyr at Philadelphia

New streamlined train will visit Eastern cities during the next three weeks

Elaborate dedicatory services for the new Burlington high-speed, streamlined train, the Zephyr, were held in the Broad Street Station of the Pennsylvania Railroad at Philadelphia, Pa., on the afternoon of Wednesday, April 18. Graham McNamee, the radio announcer, acted as master of ceremonies and in directing a broadcast over the NBC chain of radio stations. The group at the ceremony included a large number of railway and railway supply representatives, as well as many prominent citizens of Philadelphia.

The first speaker was Philip H. Gadsden, president of the Chamber of Commerce of Philadelphia. He expressed pride in the fact that the train was a product of a local manufacturer. General W. W. Atterbury, president of the Pennsylvania, was unable to attend the ceremony, but spoke from the NBC studios in Radio City, New York, congratulating President Ralph Budd of the Burlington, "whose vision, courage, initiative and genuine railroad executive ability have made this new train possible." He also congratulated the officers and employees of the various manufac-turing organizations, whose products had been used on the new train.

Edward G. Budd, president of the Edward G. Budd Manufacturing Company, was next introduced as the builder of the new train. He paid a high tribute to all those who had been instrumental in producing it, not only in his organization, but in the other companies whose products were used. He said, also, that President Budd of the Burlington had been interested in this type of equipment from the time that the Budd Company built its first sample rail car in August, 1932.

Alfred P. Sloan, president of the General Motors Corporation, whose subsidiary, the Winton Engine Corporation, designed and constructed the Diesel engine power plant, commented upon the extent to which scientific industrial research was represented in the new train. William Irvin, president of the United States Steel Corporation, spoke briefly on the development and qualities of the stainless steel. Gerard Swope, president of the General Electric Company, was unable to be present, but spoke over the radio from New York, referring in particular to the extent to which electricity in various ways was instrumental in making the train a success. Owen Cunningham, announcer for Philadelphia's radio station WLIT, then spoke from the circular glass-enclosed observation solarium at the rear end of the train, giving his impressions of the outstanding features from the stand-point of passenger comfort and convenience.

Ralph Budd, president of Burlington, thanked all those who had made the new train possible, and then indicated that after an exhibition tour, the train will operate between Kansas City, Omaha and Lincoln. "To those of us on the railroads," said Mr. Budd, "this sleek, glistening, streamlined streak symbolizes progress, and it is appropriate that the Burlington should build this train for use along the Missouri river, for Burlington was the first to reach the Missouri in the railroad race for the West. That was in 1859."

Miss Marguerite Cotsworth, a student of Swathmore College, and the daughter of Albert Cotsworth, Jr., passenger traffic manager of the Burlington, with a few appropriate words then christened the train. As the bottle crashed against the Zephyr, its siren sounded and whistles on the locomotives in the terminals added to the din. The train then proceeded on its maiden trip, a special Pennsylvania train escorting it to Paoli.

The Zephyr will make an extensive tour of the country prior to its being placed on exhibition at A Century of Progress exposition in Chicago in early July. Proceeding from Philadelphia, the train will visit principal cities of the Middle Atlantic and New England states before turning westward for visits to Middle Western points and thence to Burlington System and Pacific Coast tours. *Railway Age, April 21, 1934*

---

ployees of the Burlington Route, Electro-Motive and Winton Engine.

14-YEAR-OLD REDISKE

There was one individual, a 14-year-old boy named Robert W. Rediske, who rode the Zephyr on its record-breaking sprint. Through his memories of over 70 years past, we're privileged to join the 85 or so individuals who made the "dawn to dusk" run between Denver and Chicago.

Said Robert Rediske:

In late 1932 or early 1933 Ralph Budd decided a new train would have to grace Burlington rails. At the time I was 12 or 13 years old. My dad, Ernest A. Rediske, had worked for the Burlington Route for years and his La Cross Division office was on the second floor of the Aurora, Illinois depot. One day when I was visiting Dad, Mr. Budd was at the office, and Dad introduced me to him.

Sensing an opportunity as only a youth can, I immediately queried, " When are you going to build the new train—what will it look like?"

I do not recall Mr. Budd's answer except that with a twinkle in his eye he told my obviously embarrassed father, "Don't cuff him for being so inquisitive!"

A short while later Mr. Budd reappeared at the Division Offices and presented me with a sketch of the planned Zephyr. Using that preliminary sketch, during the summer of 1933 I carved a wooden model of the train, which proved to be rather accurate upon the arrival of the prototype in April 1934.

Ralph Budd, president of the CB&Q, waves his hat from the cab of the Pioneer Zephyr for a publicity shot near the Budd factory in North Philadelphia in April of 1934. *Chris Burritt collection*

When the model was completed, Dad temporarily requisitioned it for his office desk. He was determined to show Ralph Budd that "there was some substance" to the younger Rediske.

I pestered my father unmercifully about going on the speed run. Somehow he arranged it—perhaps the model proved more valuable than I realized. He had but one condition—that for as long as he was a Burlington employee, I was not to discuss or even mention the trip.

The silence lasted a long time—Dad was a Burlington Route employee for over 50 years.

The Zephyr was open for public exhibition on April 23-25, 1934 at Denver Union Station. A trainman friend of Dad shepherded me from Aurora to Denver over the night of the 24th and 25th, and I managed to catch a few hours of sleep on his couch the evening of the 25th.

After the Zephyr's final day of exhibition was completed, in mid-afternoon it was moved to the shops for a final going over before the trip began. About 4:00 p.m.—only 12 hours before the trip was scheduled to start at an early 4:00 a.m. (Mountain Time)—a mechanical inspector was horrified to find one of the traction motor roller bearings on CB&Q #9900's lead truck was cracked, and had to be replaced. The "Q" had no such spare part anywhere near Denver.

With the Burlington Route having spent over $50,000 of precious Depression Era cash on nationwide print and radio publicity regarding the run, and literally thousands of men, women, and children intending to be trackside the following day, the cracked

bearing instantly produced ulcers, and raised blood pressure and tempers for all concerned—except apparently Ralph Budd.

In the midst of the angst created by the bearing replacement a confident Ralph Budd told a national radio audience, "Tomorrow at dawn we'll be on our way!"

A long distance phone call to Electro-Motive confirmed they had the part in stock—but in Detroit with the better part of a week required for delivery. A frustrated employee's comment that the Union Pacific would certainly enjoy seeing their competition in difficulty set Ralph Budd thinking. He knew Union Pacific President Ralph Gray, and wasn't above giving him a call at home.

UP President Gray was most gracious: "Yes, we do have the same type bearing in our traction motors for the M-10000 train at our Omaha shops. I'll have one pulled immediately."

Accounts differ as to whether it was a UP or Burlington employee who retrieved the bearing at Omaha and boarded a scheduled flight to Cheyenne where he crossed to a chartered plane bound to Denver. Regardless of who employed the messenger, he personally handed the precious bearing over to CB&Q Assistant to the Vice President Fred Gurley at Denver airport. A police escort with sirens blaring accompanied Gurley and his cargo in their midnight race from the airport to the Burlington shops.

Lost on everybody at the time was the exquisite irony of using an airplane to save the day for the Zephyr.

REINCKE-ELLIS-YOUNGGREEN & FINN
INCORPORATED
Advertising
ESTABLISHED 1907
520 North Michigan Avenue - Chicago

JOSEPH H. FINN
VICE PRESIDENT

January 24, 1934

Mr. Albert Cotsworth, Jr.
Passenger Traffic Manager
Chicago, Burlington & Quincy Railroad
547 West Jackson Blvd.
Chicago, Illinois

My dear Mr. Cotsworth:

That the Burlington System may cash-in effectively on the unequaled opportunity offered for publicity in the projected Eastern Exhibition of The Zephyr, is the purpose of the accompanying digest.

Obviously, we are able to supply only the "high spots", else this commentary would have grown into a volume. We realize, of course, that the train is EXPERIMENTAL but after all in its dramatization is it not humanly inspiring?

The visiting crowds will not expect by the wave of a magic wand, that the expensive steam transportation of the nation will be transformed into something else, all of a sudden.

Not even the big city newspapers with their stressing of headlines have any such foolish visualization. Yes, they are interested in new things, because that is the spirit of the age, hence the newspapers "play them up".

The way of evolution, hitched to science, is a long hard journey from the box-like contraption the Dayton brothers flew only a hundred feet or so at Kitty Hawk (when I was a cub reporter) to the plane Lindbergh used to span the Atlantic.

But epochs are epochs and leadership is leadership and here is another beginning that may mean much measured in years ahead - not a mere cycle of days.

In arranging this Eastern tour of The Zephyr may I presume to say that you supplied a notable vehicle for constructive publicity.

With such a beginning, perhaps you will excuse the enthusiasm in the pages that follow. However, I feel frankly like this—here is a great opportunity—let's use it effectively for the Burlington.

Sincerely yours,
Joseph H. Finn

The Reincke-Ellis-Younggreen & Finn publicity plan for the Zephyr began with these enthusiastic words.

A PLAN TO MAKE THE EASTERN TRIP OF THE ZEPHYR A BUSINESS BUILDER FOR THE BURLINGTON SYSTEM
NO WESTERN RAILROAD EVER HAD THIS OPPORTUNITY

Let us look at this projected trip of The Zephyr, not just as an exhibition of a single revolutionary type train, but as an unparalleled opportunity to register Burlington LEADERSHIP and to present to successive crowds in these centers of population the big good will building story of the Burlington System.

No Western Railroad in our judgment, has ever had a setting just like this in which to promote your product-service both passenger and freight EVERYWHERE WEST.

Therefore, we urge—let's make the most of it and let's overlook no single incident (within reason) that will contribute to the complete picture.

While the exhibition of the Royal Scot supplied the precedent for the Zephyr's swing around the East, the significance of the latter completely overshadows the visit of the Britisher.

The difference between the Scot and conventional Steam Equipment was only in detail—revolutionary is the contrast between the Zephyr and present users of the rails.

Your competitor (UP) at the present writing is confining his exhibition to Chicago and the West, while you will show the Zephyr in that section of the U.S.A. which has 70% population.

Interest in this new type train is at its height as evidenced by the fact that newspapers on metropolitan cities and elsewhere are utilizing the material sent out by ourselves and Mr. McLaury have published columns of pictures and write-ups since the initial announcements.

Thousands of clippings have come in from every corner of the country.

Editorials have appeared in countless journals hailing this type of train as the answer to the problem of the carriers, winning back lost passenger travel and as a challenge to the air.

We have a background here inviting further skillful promotion to make "The Zephyr" tour of the East the most notable event since the first appearance of the "Iron Horse" or Fulton's demonstration of the first steamboat on the Hudson River. The appearance of The Zephyr in these great centers of population should prove a veritable sensation, and we urge that no reasonable stone be left unturned to translate this interest into profitable business for the entire Burlington System.

At the General Electric plant in Schenectady, New York on April 28, 1934, the Zephyr poses with the many men who worked to develop the entirely new electrical system of the diesel-electric streamliner.

With the power car's nose up on jacks, the traction motor bearing was carefully—but hurriedly—installed, the power truck replaced under the train and with a collective sigh of relief, #9900 slowly departed the shops for Union Station. The 4:00 a.m. starting time came and went.

Amidst all the sweaty-palmed "Q" and supplier executives awaiting word that the Zephyr was ready for boarding, there was one passenger who cared not one whit. That was "Zeph," purportedly the burro mascot of the University of Colorado. How he got aboard the speed run is a story in itself of Ralph Budd's skill at combining humor, opportunism and self-promotion.

Although this story has been repeated in various forms over the years*, this is the version I personally heard from Ralph Budd's lips. I was in my father's office waiting to go to lunch with him and Aurora Yardmaster Ed Ready.

It was just prior to the speed run and Budd was bemoaning the fact that, "With my proverbial neck on the line the Western newspapers aren't giving the story enough space or credence."

Ed Ready commented, "You could make the Western folks a lot happier and gain some brownie points by offering to transport the (University of) Colorado mascot to Kansas City for the big game."

Budd stated, "This is a nonstop trip."

"So, no one would know the difference if the mascot went to Kansas City by way of Chicago."

Budd queried, "What kind of mascot?"

"A Colorado Canary—a burro."

After a definite pause Budd responded with considerable understatement,

"Why not, one more jackass on this trip won't make any difference!"

———

* There are several published versions of this story. One claims that Zeph was a gift from the Mayor of Denver to the Mayor of Chicago for the fair. Another states the exchange occurred in the Denver shops during the evening before the run between the editor of the Rocky Mountain News and Burlington Route Vice President Ed Flynn. Regardless of the particulars, the punch line remains the same!

———

Finally, by 5:02 a.m on Track One at Denver Union Station the Zephyr was filled with its cargo of notables, including Ralph Budd, CB&Q; Edward Budd, Budd Co.; Harold Hamilton, EMC; and "Zeph." Among the 85 or so men aboard, I was virtually unnoticed sitting on a telegrapher's stool in the baggage compartment.

A green flag used to start the prior 11 Indianapolis 500 auto races was ceremoniously dropped by Mr. C. J. Ince, general manager, Mountain Division, Western Union Telegraph Company, to inaugurate our trip. Superintendent of Automotive Equipment Ernest Weber released the air brakes with a hiss, and slowly notched out the quadrant throttle. The Winton engine's grumbling at idle grew over the next seconds to a full

This was another publicity photo taken of the Pioneer Zephyr for the sake of the railroad, Western Union and the Railway Express Agency. The Zephyr's average speed of 79.1 miles per hour between Denver and Harvard, Nebraska set a world record in 1934.

throated roar, and the Zephyr moved forward, slicing the Western Union timing tape at precisely 5:04:40 Mountain Standard Time, recording the official start of the 1,015.4-mile run.

Zeph: Fastest Burro

A few feet away from me was Zeph, the soon-to-be fastest burro in history, contentedly munching on a hay bale. Unfortunately, as the trip progressed, speed did not agree with Zeph, and he brayed incessantly, creating headaches for most everyone in the baggage area.

Also in the baggage compartment was Wayne Wigton. A classmate of mine at Aurora's East High School, Wayne was the wireless radio operator. His job was to keep the dispatchers informed as to the train's location along the main line through the use of Morse code. Wayne was an accomplished short-wave operator, having acquired his radio license at 11 years of age. Now, a freshly-minted high school graduate of 17, he was pioneering a never-before-tried railroad communication system he had personally set up. He had confidence in his system, as he previously had regularly communicated with ham radio operators in Denver.

Wigton's on-board equipment consisted of a Morse code key, a radio transmitter and a receiver with earphones to hear incoming messages. All equipment fit on one small table. Three 12" high antennas spaced 22' apart had been mounted to the roof of the Zephyr for signal transmission. The radio signals Wayne sent were received at his ham radio receiver in his home in Aurora, Illinois. Two licensed ham radio friends of Wayne manned his home station during the trip just in case something went amiss. The signal traveled from there by wire down the street to the dispatcher's office in the Burlington's Aurora depot. Updates were transcribed by the CB&Q dispatcher and relayed over the Burlington system by conventional telegraph wire from Aurora.

Wayne Wigton's only problem on the trip developed when the crate containing Zeph fell over as the Zephyr rounded a curve at high speed. The braying burro was unhurt, but Wayne received a nasty scar on his leg in the process.

For his efforts Wayne earned the princely sum of $0.52 per hour.

Wayne Wigton's successful radiotelegraphy during the Zephyr trip was just the beginning of his 43-year career with the Burlington. He retired from Burlington Northern as communications director in 1977 and died December 15, 1984.

Getting far more attention in the crowded, noisy baggage compartment was T. Wigton, Wayne's father. A career Burlington employee, he was computing the train's speed by

1934
THREE DAY PROGRAM OF
THE BURLINGTON ZEPHYR IN PHILADELPHIA

TUESDAY - April 17th — Press Preview Day at the Budd Plant, North Philadelphia, 9:00 A.M., for the convenience of newspaper reporters, newspaper cameramen and motion picture operators.

WEDNESDAY - April 18th — Ceremonial Day, 2:30 to 3:00 P.M., including Christening of the Burlington Zephyr, at the Broad Street Station. This half hour between 2:30 and 3:00 P.M. includes NBC chain broadcast. Also, broadcast NBC chain 4:00 to 4:30 while the Zephyr, accompanied by Pennsylvania steam escort train, is enroute from Broad Street Station to Paoli and Downingtown.

Preceding the ceremonies in the afternoon and from 9:00 A.M. to 11:00 A.M. there will be two runs with the Zephyr, unescorted, first to Paoli and return, and second, to Downingtown and return. All three trips on Wednesday will be for invited guests only.

THURSDAY - April 19th — Public Exhibition of the Burlington Zephyr for 8:30 A.M. to 9:00 P.M. at the Broad Street Station.

OUTSTANDING FEATURES OF
THE PIONEER ZEPHYR

• America's first diesel-powered, streamline train, capable of a speed in excess of 100 miles an hour.

• The Zephyr is built of stainless steel—weighs approximately one hundred tons, only a little more than a single standard Pullman sleeper.

• It is air-conditioned throughout, with temperature thermostatically-controlled. Windows sealed and equipped with non-shatter glass.

• The power plant is a 660 horsepower, eight-in-line, diesel engine, burning oil...a safety factor. This power plant requires neither spark plug nor carburetor.

• Not a single rivet is used from bow to stern. Metal is joined with a new process known as Shotwelding through electric "stitches." A more efficient substitute thus has been found for conventional riveting.

• The Burlington Zephyr comprises three cars articulated, as contrasted with the conventional vestibuled connections between cars.

• The first car contains the engine room and compartments for the handling of U.S. Mail, there being a substantial amount of mail on the particular run for which the Zephyr was built.

• The second car includes an area for express matter, plus a buffet grill and space accommodations set apart for smokers.

• The main body of the rear or third car is devoted to paired seats, adjustable from normal upright position to a semi-reclining angle. This third car has a parlor observation end, fitted like a solarium with safety glass throughout to afford clear vision.

• Meals supplied direct from the electric buffet grill to occupants of chairs. A removable table can be bracketed between the seats for dining and other utility purposes.

• All passenger compartments of the train equipped for radio reception.

• Sixteen wheels altogether under the Zephyr...trucks located at front and rear and under articulation between first and second car and second and third car, insuring smooth riding qualities, less noise and elimination of what is called unpleasant "jolting" due to "slack" between cars of an ordinary train. The conventional train of like capacity has thirty-six wheels instead of sixteen as under the Zephyr.

• Each of the four-wheel trucks under the Zephyr is rubber-cushioned at thirty-two points. The wheels are solid steel alloy with integral tread, rim-toughened to render long service without regrinding or replacement. All axles are equipped with roller bearings.

• The Zephyr, because of its stainless steel construction, is not painted exteriorly. This stainless steel consists of 18% chromium and 8% nickel, cold-rolled, and characterized by its light weight, great ruggedness, high tensile strength, resistance to fatigue, plus non-corrosive qualities which render painting unnecessary.

• The framework of the train embodies the scientific latticed method of construction, with plates and parts secured through electric Shotwelding. Each "shot" of electric current is precisely timed, resulting in absolute uniformity in welds, which occur as close together as the stitches in a seam, unifying the sections effectually without breakdown of the molecular unity of the metal.

• Unlike the conventional railroad car and automobile body, the structure of the Zephyr's three units does not rest upon a frame or sill. Points of contact with the trucks of the Zephyr are exceedingly steady—the members or piers are built integral with the ends of each car—the method of construction being comparable to that of a bridge.

• All horizontal and vertical stress members and weight-sustaining parts in the new train's framework consist of U-shaped struts and beams for maximum strength combined with light weight.

• A new type of insulation invented for the Zephyr.... a metal foil almost as thin as tissue paper... it is slightly crumbled before being placed in position. Only one hundred pounds of this newly-invented insulation is used in the entire train.

• Super-safety air brake equipment. With hand and foot of operator off controls, the train automatically comes to a stop. The air brake equipment controls the rate of retardation to prevent sliding wheels.

• The center of gravity of the Zephyr is 51 inches above the rails (approximately 20% lower than conventional passenger equipment). This novel train, therefore, "hugs the rails," and has requisite balance, with avoidance of swaying action when rounding curves.

• The Zephyr was built at the North Philadelphia plant of the E. G. Budd Manufacturing Co. Paul Cret, the eminent architect, was consulting designer on the interior for the builders, and the Chicago firm of Holabird & Root for the Burlington Railroad.

checking mileposts with a stopwatch and the various newspaper reporters constantly wanted updates.

Although the Zephyr's reported top speed was 112.5 mph, both Wayne and his father insisted for years an omission had occurred and that the top speed actually reached was 122.5 mph. Unfortunately, the speedometer couldn't confirm the stopwatch, as it went no higher than 120 mph.

As the eastbound Zephyr roared into the rising sun, speed was kept down to a leisurely 60-80 mph for the first 100 miles or so to allow the new bearings to "seat in" and not overheat. Still, it only took 68.5 minutes to cover the 78 miles from Denver to Fort Collins, Colorado.

The Zephyr was operated between Denver and Chicago by three teams of men. Each team consisted of a motorman who actually operated the throttle; a maintenance engineer who sat in the "fireman's" seat on the left side of the cab separated from the motorman by the generator; and a division road foreman of engines who sat directly behind the motorman on a makeshift jump seat and knew the particular section of track being covered like the back of his hand. All were hand-picked by senior management, who also authorized the division managers to pay the union brothers their day's wages without question, who would have otherwise worked the train based upon seniority.

Motormen Take Shifts

Jack Ford, Ernie Kuehn and Ernest Weber were the three motormen who took shifts at the throttle of the Zephyr between Denver and Chicago. Ford and Webber were Burlington men, Ford was a road foreman of engines and Weber was superin-

tendent of automotive equipment. Ernie Kuehn was on Electro-Motive's payroll as a field engineer and had been since 1926.

Weber was at the throttle from Denver to Akron, Nebraska, where Ford relieved him. Kuehn took over at McCook, and Weber began his second round at Hastings. Ford returned to the throttle at Lincoln while Kuehn relieved him at Creston, Iowa. Weber's final service at the throttle was from Ottumwa to Galesburg, Illinois, where Ford took charge from there to Chicago and—assisted by an Illinois Central pilot—down the lakefront on the ICRR and onto the Century of Progress fairground itself.

The changing of motormen at speed was precisely choreographed so that the "deadman's pedal" would always have a motorman's foot on it. Without the weight of a foot it would rise and automatically engage the air brakes, bringing the Zephyr to a halt.

The non-stop trip nearly ended before it had really begun. Somehow an access door slammed on an instrument wire, and the resulting short circuit burned through the engine starter cable. Smelling burning rubber, Jack Ford, who was operating the train at the time, shut down the diesel engine.

When the incident occurred the Zephyr was traveling down a 40-mile descending grade. For long minutes the train coasted quietly toward a seemingly certain stop while the speed slowly decreased to 15 mph and technicians unsuccessfully tried to splice the starter cable. Ralph Budd rushed from his post in the observation lounge to the cab to see what the problem was. In an act of selfless desperation, EMC Technician Roy Baer grabbed and held the cable ends together with his bare hands. Jack Ford hit the starter button—there was an electrical flash at the bare cable ends in Baer's hands—and the Winton engine

roared to life. All was well except for Roy Baer's hands, which were badly burned.

Low Air Pressure

Later that afternoon as Burlington Engineer Ernest Weber was operating the Zephyr through Burlington, Iowa, the extensive use of the air brakes down West Burlington hill and whistling for the numerous city grade crossings nearly brought the special to a halt. Air pressure was so low it began to trigger an automatic—and unwanted—brake application. EMC Field Engineer Ernie Kuehn realized what the cause of the problem was, reached over Weber's shoulder, and yanked the throttle back. The wide open engine speeded up the air compressor, refilled the system air tanks and kept the non-stop run intact.

And what a non-stop run it was. The Zephyr averaged 90 miles per hour for 129.5 consecutive miles, 106.2 mph for 19.1 miles, and 109 mph for 6.4 miles. The speedometer hit 112.5 mph between Yuma and Schramm, Colorado, while at one location train speed was calculated to be 122.5 mph via mileposts and a stopwatch. For many on board it was the fastest ride of their lives.

Engineer Jack Ford wrote a brief two column article for the following day's (Sunday) edition of the New York Times in which he commented, " It looked as though every person in each of the 164 towns—as well as rural areas the Zephyr passed through—had the entire population out [trackside] to see the record run."

Ford wasn't far off. An estimated half million Americans watched and cheered the God of the West Wind as it streaked

Log of the Zephyr

(The time is Denver Standard)

Station	Miles from Denver.	Time.	Elapsed Time.
Left Denver		5:04:40 a.m.	....
Yuma, Colo	137.5	7:00:08 a.m.	1 hr. 55 min. 28 sec.
McCook, Neb	254.3	8:19:50 a.m.	3 hrs. 15 min. 10 sec.
Harvard, Neb	401.5	11:09:00 a.m.	5 hrs. 4 min. 20 sec.
Lincoln, Neb	482.6	11:12:15 a.m.	6 hrs. 7 min. 35 sec.
Ashland, Neb	507.0	11:31:00 a.m.	6 hrs. 26 min. 20 sec.
Corning, Ia	603.7	12:56:32 p.m.	7 hrs. 51min. 50 sec.
Ottumwa, Ia	737.7	2:43:15 p.m.	9 hrs. 38 min. 35 sec.
Mt. Pleasant, Ia	784.2	3:17:45 p.m.	10 hrs. 13 min. 5 sec.
Monmouth, Ill	838.3	4:00:30 p.m.	10 hrs. 55 min. 50 sec.
Kewanee, Ill	886.4	4:38:00 p.m.	11 hrs. 33 min. 20 sec.
Earlville, Ill	945.3	5:18:00 p.m.	12 hrs 13 min. 20 sec.
Chicago	1,015.4	7:09:44 p.m.	13 hrs. 5 min. 4 sec.
Average speed			77.58 miles an hour

The Log of the Zephyr speed trip, breaking the record time into segments, first appeared on the front page of the Denver Post the following day. The city/town location breakdown was undoubtedly done in concert with Wayne Wigton's father charting elapsed time via a stop watch. Log statistics were dropped off by Wigton at pre-determined locations. Elapsed mileage is broken down into tenths. Both elapsed time as well as the time the Zephyr "went through" was charted to the minute and second.
Courtesy Denver Post

Boston's South Station was the scene of this welcoming crowd for the Pioneer Zephyr as part of its 25-city publicity tour on April 26, 1934. *J. Michael Gruber collection*

past. They added a new expression to the American lexicon in the process: "She sure is coming—wasn't she!"

At 7:09:44 p.m. Central Standard Time the Zephyr broke the timing tape at Halsted Street in Chicago, exactly 13 hours and five minutes after leaving Denver. The 1,015.4-mile trip had been completed at an average speed of 77.6 mph, a new world record.

One hour later, at 8:09 p.m. the Zephyr rolled to a stop on the stage of Edward Hungerford's "Wings of a Century" pageant, officially opening the second year of the Chicago Century of Progress Exposition. A tumultuous crowd estimated in excess of 10,000 poured from the stands to enthusiastically welcome and examine the newly-arrived Zephyr.

Amidst the fair's hoopla I departed the Zephyr, caught a taxi to Union Station, and took a late evening commuter train home to Aurora and a good night's sleep.

The Zephyr's 13 hour, five minute 1,015-mile trip clearly established that the fuel economy, thermal efficiency, and stamina exhibited by the new GM/Winton two-stroke cycle diesel engine meant it was ready for the railroad world. That "straight eight" Winton engine had consumed only $16.72 worth of $0.04-per-gallon furnace oil, as diesel fuel was then called. Some 418 gallons of oil

were burned, averaging 2.43 miles per gallon at the amazing average speed of nearly 78 mph. Orders would soon start arriving at Electro-Motive and Winton, as well as Budd.

THUNDEROUS WELCOME

After its thunderous welcome, CB&Q #9900 had all of one day to rest up at the Century of Progress Exhibition in Chicago before continuing on with its tour. Proving just how much the Burlington's speed run had caught the public's attention, 15,757 people queued up to visit the stainless steel speedster on Sunday, May 27, 1934.

Over the next three weeks the Zephyr toured many Western U.S. cities. On June 16 it led three freight trains over the newly-completed 38-mile-long Dotsero Cutoff between Bond (Dotsero) and Orestod, Colorado. The cutoff allowed Denver & Rio Grande Western trains from Utah to directly access Denver via the 6.2-mile-long Moffat Tunnel saving 175 miles over the original Royal Gorge Route via Tennessee Pass and Pueblo.

Upon completion of its Los Angeles and San Francisco visits, CB&Q #9900 returned to Chicago in mid-July, and except for a quick roundtrip to the Twin Cities on July 30

On its exhibition journey through the East in 1934, the Pioneer Zephyr slides through Weston, New Jersey on the Reading RR, "stopped" by the camera at 100 miles an hour.

to help the Operating Department develop a schedule for its abuilding twin sisters, basked in its internal combustion and streamlined success for the remainder of the fair. Its Union Pacific rival, M-10000, also spent most of the summer at the fair as well.

After Labor Day the Zephyr warmed up its Winton engine and again headed west—this time to become a movie star. RKO Studios in Hollywood took exterior shots of the streamliner, now unimaginatively renamed the Silver Streak, on location between September 7 and October 9. Locations used were on the "Q", Denver & Rio Grande Western, and—interestingly enough—the Union Pacific.

The 72-minute film cost $122,000 to produce, played to receptive national audiences, and ultimately turned a profit—albeit small—for RKO Studios. Perhaps the less said the better regarding the movie's plot. It involved a stainless steel streamliner, a railroad president's beautiful daughter, an Iron Lung—the latest in 1934 medical science—and a German spy trying to steal the secrets of the new two-cycle diesel engine. Trains magazine columnist Wally Abby summed it up best when he wrote, " All characters, including the train, lived happily ever after" (excepting, of course, the spy).

SILVER STREAK TODAY

Silver Streak remains available today on video and speaks volumes about the changes in sophistication, transportation and medicine that America has undergone in the past three quarters of a century.

(In the mid-'70's Hollywood released a second *Silver Streak*. A comedy starring Richard Prior and Gene Wilder, it bore no relationship to the original except in name, and that the action occurred on Budd-built stainless steel streamline passenger cars.)

With its movie debut pending and having been visited by 2,016,606 people during its 30,437 mile, 222 cities tour between April 18 and November 10, 1934, the Burlington Zephyr was finally ready to begin providing the service for which it was purchased.

Making an unofficial speed run of 131 miles an hour, the Pioneer Zephyr nears Amarillo, Texas, whizzing past elevators, road crossings and telephone poles at a break-neck pace.

Memorandum of Plan for Handling the Engine of the Zephyr on May 26th – Denver to Chicago

1. It is assumed that the Road Foremen and the Train Crew, as well as Messrs. Weber, Ford, Kuehn and the Maintenance Engineers have read the memorandum of the meeting held at Chicago, May 12th. They should particularly note requirements on Page 2 about the possibility of picking up others enroute. (Consider and decide how train crew will know about an order to be picked up. I think we had better have the Road Foreman in the front end telephone the employees in the baggage car about it). Suggestion is that if we pick up any order enroute we should slow down even slower than the 30 miles outlined on Page 2 in order to insure against having to stop account missing order and, furthermore, if any one set of orders is picked up that will be sufficient. Train crews should also note instructions about slow downs where messages may be picked up. We will not stop for any messages which may be missed at these points.

2. Train orders and Clearances are to be delivered to the retrospective Conductor and Brakeman-Flagman and to the Road Foreman of Engines.

3. The actual operation of the engine shall be alternately by Messrs. Weber, Ford and Kuehn. These motormen will be paired with "Maintenance Engineers" and these teams shall operate as follows:

Weber - Clarke	Denver to Akron	111.42 Miles	1'20"
Ford - Murphy	Akron to McCook	142.95 Miles	1'40"
Kuehn - Piper	McCook to Hastings	131.67 Miles	1'40"
Weber - Clarke	Hastings to Lincoln	96.54 Miles	1'10"
Ford - Murphy	Lincoln to Creston	141.72 Miles	2'00"
Kuehn - Frame	Creston to Ottumwa	113.3 Miles	1'30"
Weber - Clarke	Ottumwa to Galesburg	117.3 Miles	1'30"
Ford - Murphy	Galesburg to Chicago	160.0 Miles	2'10"

The Road Foreman shall be seated on the right hand side of the cab immediately behind the motorman.

The "Maintenance Engineer" will be seated immediately to the left of the motorman. The motorman and the Maintenance Engineer before going "on duty" will go over with each other the speed restrictions in the territory covered by their assignment so that they will have a thorough understanding before they assume "control". It will be the obligation of the "Maintenance Engineer" to call to the motorman all speed restrictions and it shall be the obligation of the motorman to call back the speed restrictions so there will be no possibility for misunderstanding. The Maintenance Engineer will use for his guidance an especially prepared profile and alignment chart which has been put in books according to subdivisions. i.e., Denver-Akron, Akron-McCook, etc. The Road Foreman will be furnished with a type-written list of all speed restrictions. Unless, however, the Maintenance Engineer fails to call proper slow indication it will not be necessary for the Road Foreman to do so, the underlying idea being that it is much better for the motorman to have his speed restrictions called by only one person. The Road Foreman is, however, to carefully observe all signals, crossings, crowds at station platforms, etc. Also, he will take whatever action is necessary to insure safety in any situation when, in his judgment, the motorman does not function as he should. The Road Foreman shall secure a stop-watch from officers supplied with them. He will make sufficient checks of the time consumed between mile posts to know whether the speed-indicator is accurate and, if not accurate, he will post the motorman. If the speed recorder should fail he will keep track of the speed by the use of his stop-watch. (Perhaps we should furnish the motorman with a stop-watch to be used in such a circumstance—Consider and decide). *Museum of Science and Industry archives*

It was important for the Burlington to take extra precautions in the handling of the non-stop Denver to Chicago Pioneer Zephyr run on May 26. Part of a Burlington Railroad memorandum to employees shows how careful the preparations for the trip were.

Memorandum of meeting at Chicago Saturday, May 12, 1934, with reference to non-stop movement of the Zephyr Denver to Chicago Saturday, May 26, 1934.

```
Leave Denver.................................................4:00 A.M. (M.T.)
Arrive Chicago Fair Grounds not later than....................7:30 P.M. (CST)
Time distribution charts will be mailed to all concerned a little later.
```

Operate as Second No. 6 Denver to Ashland, as No. 34 Ashland to Oreapolis, as Second No. 6 Oreapolis to Burlington, and as Second No. 18 from Burlington to Chicago.

Mr. Shults and the Superintendents concerned are to immediately confer with the Division Officers and the Trick Dispatchers who will be in charge of dispatching when the Zephyr moves, and clearly outline just how orders are to be handled. The plan is that the Road Foremen who are mentioned in the latter part of this memorandum will take necessary orders for the Zephyr to Denver and then, if there is no wire failure, the Dispatchers will cut through to Denver the evening of May 25, 1934, at which time the Dispatchers will again check the clearances and orders for the Zephyr.

In addition to temporary slow orders, the Zephyr leaving Denver should receive orders from each Division to the effect that "No Orders For Your Train at Akron" and all other similar situations where there are train order offices not equipped with train order signals.

Orders should also be issued instructing the crew of the Zephyr not to register at register stations.

Run-late orders should be issued and, generally, these run-lates should break only at subdivision points.

ON SINGLE TRACK, opposing passenger and freight trains shall make their own meeting point with the Zephyr, based upon the run-late order. Passenger trains shall be required to clear the time of the Zephyr at least thirty minutes. Opposing freight trains will be in the clear two hours in advance of the time the Zephyr is due on the sub-division as established by run-late order. It is important that train and enginemen be interviewed personally by competent officer and, in addition, an officer should be on each passenger train which makes its own meeting point with the Zephyr.

Extreme care should be used in protecting passengers and others on trains which are on siding to meet the Zephyr. Vestibules should be closed to prevent people stepping out in front of the Zephyr

ON SINGLE TRACK, passenger trains and freight trains in the same direction shall clear the Zephyr in the same manner as outlined for opposing trains, except that, unless there be quite unusual circumstances, the entire subdivision shall be cleared of freight trains ahead of the Zephyr.

ON DOUBLE TRACK, the Zephyr is to operate on the eastward track and each sub-division will be cleared of freight and passenger trains at least two hours before the Zephyr is due to enter that sub-division. On double track, all trains will be required to stand while the Zephyr passes. The Dispatcher shall instruct trains at what place they are to stand still under such circumstances. It is desired that,

generally, trains will stand just outside station limits at locations instructed by the Dispatcher.

It is desired to have some officer ride the trains and, while standing, carefully inspect the side of their train to see that there is nothing protruding that will interfere with the safe passage of the Zephyr. This inspection should also be made on single track and in the territory East of Aurora.

EAST OF AURORA, use middle track Aurora to Union Street Tower, where crossover movement is to be made onto St. Charles Air Line.

Superintendents and Chief Dispatchers to be in Dispatchers' office keeping in intimate touch with the progress of the train over their Division. Mr. Haines should be at Creston. The Superintendents and Chief Dispatchers should insure that the Dispatchers do not take any liberties with the Zephyr and, except in the case of an extreme emergency, do not attempt to issue any orders to the Zephyr. If there should be some unexpected emergency situation which makes it necessary to issue orders to the Zephyr after leaving Denver, give the crew of the Zephyr advice one train order station in advance that at the following train order station they must slow down to pick up orders. For example, if it should become necessary to pick up orders at Benkelman, advice will be furnished the Zephyr passing Parks. In order to handle this quickly and uniformly the operator at Parks is to be instructed to have his train order signal in a clear position and to stand on the platform holding a lantern in his right hand at arm's length above his head. Under these circumstances, the crew of the Zephyr will approach the next train order office at a speed of thirty miles per hour where two sets of train orders will be delivered as follows:

(a) Engine room,
(b) Passenger doorway of the second car.
(Another trainman will be stationed in the passenger doorway of the third unit to pick up the orders in case any of the others have missed their order).

The Zephyr will slow down to:

·25 miles per hour at the Hastings-Nebraska shoo fly,
·35 miles per hour through Lincoln passenger yard,
·25 miles per hour around 12-degree curve at Plattsmouth,
·25 miles per hour over Main Street crossing at Burlington,
·35 miles per hour over railroad crossing in Mendota yard.

Any messages for officers on the Zephyr may be sent to those stations. Train crew will be prepared to pick up messages on station platform side at Hastings, Nebraska; Lincoln, and

Burlington; on the right hand side at the 12-degree curve at Plattsmouth; and on the right hand side at Mendota.

The engine will be operated alternately by Messrs. Kuehn, Weber, and Ford. Road Foremen from the following Divisions shall arrive in Denver not later than No. 3 the morning of May 25 and accompany train and act as pilot:

McCook Division,
Lincoln-Omaha Divisions,
Creston-Ottumwa Divisions,
Aurora-Chicago Divisions.

These motormen and pilots, as well as the conductor and flagman, are to be provided with time distribution charts which shall contain all speed restrictions, including those which may be necessary by reason of some temporary slow order. The permanent and temporary speed restrictions should be carefully checked over by the Division Officers. The time distribution charts in final form will be prepared by and delivered to the crew of the Zephyr personally by the General Manager.

Conductors shall be selected according to their ability and deadheaded to arrive in Denver not later than No. 3 the morning of May 25. Four conductors shall be provided, one each from the following divisions: McCook, Lincoln-Omaha, Creston-Ottumwa, Aurora-Chicago. Mr. Thiehoff may later decide to use only one conductor for the Lines East.

Two selected flagmen are to be deadheaded to Denver to arrive there not later than No. 3 the morning of May 25, one to be selected from Lines West and one from Lines East.

Mr. Thiehoff is to arrange meeting with the General Chairman to work out equitable and uniform plan of paying claims of enginemen who are first out and who would ordinarily be used on such train, and also work out similar situation with respect to trainmen.

Assistant Superintendents, Trainmasters, Master Mechanics, Roadmasters and all other officers are to be distributed to the best advantage. Any special officers such as Transportation Inspectors or any Staff Officers are to be available for any work in connection with the movement of this train. It is understood that Division and General Superintendents will call upon the General Manager and Vice President for any special men who, in their opinion, are needed to safely and properly handle this movement.

Flagmen shall be provided at all road crossings, both public and private, including crossings protected by crossing gates and wig wags. At important crossings where view is not good, provide at least two flagmen. These special flagmen at all road crossings shall be interviewed personally by competent officer. This officer should be first impressed with his obligation to thoroughly line up his flagmen in such a way so that they will stop traffic. We will provide a "Bell cord" rope for each side of the track at every crossing and that there be three red flags fastened to each rope. Mr. Murphy will arrange to supply necessary rope and red flags. The exact number to be supplied should be considered and decided upon at the meetings which Mr. Murphy and the others are to hold, starting at Aurora Monday morning, May 14. Posts are to be driven in the ground well in advance of the arrival of the Zephyr and immediately before the Zephyr arrives ropes shall be pulled across the highway. Special STOP signs made of heavy cardboard will be furnished for each flagman (Mr. Murphy will supply these to Superintendents). Preliminary check indicates 1070 public and 619 private crossings between Denver and Chicago, in addition to certain crossings between Galesburg and Chicago which are now provided with "24-hour gate protection".

In connection with the meetings which Mr. Murphy and Mr. Pratt are to hold with local officers, utmost care should be excerised to get the perfect lineup about protecting crowds at stations. It is considered good judgment to allow no crowd to get closer to the track than the back line of the station platform—the farther back the better. Someone should be delegated to move up and down the track to prevent people from crowding against track at locations some little distance from the station. Support of local police and State Highway police should be solicited. Some protection must also be provided when train passes under bridges, viaducts, etc., to guard against people throwing rocks onto the top of the train. This has been very noticeable in the east—in fact, one rock was thrown which struck just below the window in front of the operator.

Make definite lineup that through route is arranged for at all interlocking plants. Then, in addition to making that advance lineup, have a signal maintainer at each interlocking plant to insure that no train or any line receives a route which will conflict with movement of the Zephyr. It is especially important to check carefully the few plants where operators are employed by other lines. No freight trains will be allowed to make movements through the plant within thirty minutes of the arrival of the Zephyr and no passenger train will be allowed to move through the plant within fifteen minutes of the arrival of the Zephyr. In connection with this routing at interlocking plants, it is absolutely imperative that the men at the crossing keep in close touch with the Dispatcher and know just when the Zephyr is to arrive. They are not to depend on the time distribution charts, because it is anticipated that the Zephyr will make up some time under favorable circumstances, and there must be no failure to have a through route at all interlocking plants.

Note speed limits proposed through automatic interlocking plants. Here, again, signal maintainer must be used and he must keep signals of conflicting route set against trains, thus insuring through route for Zephyr. Signal maintainer also shall arrange to give clear indication to Zephyr well in advance of arrival because, under speeds proposed through these plants, the Zephyr will move too fast to be governed by clear signal actuated only by approach circuits. At each automatic interlocking plant, it is imperative that the man at the crossing keep in touch with the Dispatcher as outlined for other interlocking plants. In addition to the man at the crossing, there must also be two flagmen used, whose duty will be to stop trains on conflicting routes before they have fouled the bonded section of the train, which would actuate signals on the route to be used by the Zephyr. Between now and May 26, get all tracks and bridges in best possible condition, eliminating if possible all temporary slow orders. It is highly important that between now and May 26 curves be gone over to the greatest possible extent and elevation established in a uniform manner. We will be running faster on curves than is ordinarily done and uniformity of elevation is very important. No track work to be done on May 26 which would have any effect upon the safe and comfortable passage of the Zephyr. For example, on that day it is suggested no ties be inserted until after the Zephyr has passed.

Switches that will not be used for transportation purposes, such as beet sidings, are to be spiked. All facing point spring switches are to be spiked. In special cases, such as remotely controlled switches at Oxford Junction and Cobb, the facing point switches are to be spiked.

The track is to be patrolled in such manner that the patrolling will be completed one hour before the Zephyr is scheduled to enter the operating sub-division. When section men are instructed about this part of their obligation, it should be made clear to them that the Zephyr may be somewhat ahead of the schedule shown on the time distribution charts. In addition to this, on double track and three track territory inspection shall be made from motor car operated on track which will not be utilized by the Zephyr. Motor cars on May 26 are not to be set off at the usual "hand car setoff" but are to be placed at road crossings or in other locations where greater clearance can be provided. They should be thoroughly anchored, so there shall be no possibility of motor car fouling main track. After proper patrol has been made, no motor car shall operate until after the Zephyr has passed. It is important that Superintendents prepare a list of motor car operators and insure that each operator is interviewed and advised accordingly.

In connection with Burlington-Iowa drawbridge, Mr. Newton is to arrange with proper river navigation officers to keep river craft away from the bridge two hours in advance of the scheduled arrival of the Zephyr and the bridge tender will be instructed not to open the drawbridge within two hours of the scheduled time of the Zephyr. In addition to this, Mr. Grisinger is to arrange for two motor boats to patrol the river in order to police the situation, and he is also to have very clear understanding with the drawbridge operator.

Mr. Newton will also make definite lineup about guarding against conflict with river craft at the bridge on the St. Charles Air Line.

Make definite line up at points like Lincoln and Ashland where switches are operated manually to insure that they are set and then either spiked or locked well in advance of the Zephyr movement.

In case it should be necessary to stop the Zephyr by flag, flagmen should be instructed to allow a braking distance in excess of a mile, the more the better, but not less than one mile.

Trip will be made over the St. Charles Air Line Monday, May 14, and Illinois Central officers will be advised about our plans and their cooperation solicited. Mr. Flak shall personally supervise and police the situation on May 26 to insure that there is a proper line up for immediate movement of the Zephyr onto and across the St. Charles Air Line. He is also to see to it that the Illinois Central officers have necessary crews available at Illinois Central station to get the Zephyr across

Illinois Central main lines, permitting movement down to the south end of the Exposition Grounds. Mr. Falk is also to make special arrangement about washing the hoppers of the Zephyr when it stops near Illinois Central station prior to the reverse movement toward the south end of the Exposition Grounds. Mr. Falk is also to confer and cooperate with Messrs. McLaury and Cotsworth and, through them, contact necessary authorities at A Century of Progress to the end that perfect line up is made to permit the Zephyr to pass through the Wings of a Century at proper moment and, subsequently, come back to its own track south of the Transportation Building.

Mr. Beasley should provide food for all people accompanying the train. Thermos bottles and thermos jugs will be utilized because it would be impractical to cook food for such a large number on the run. Paper cups, plates, etc., will be used. It is impossible to say now how many people will be on the train, but that can be checked up at Denver the day before. A preliminary guess at this time is about 30 or 35.

A good supply of cardboard message containers will be taken along in order that people on the train can drop off messages enroute.

Dispatchers to send a pink wire, which is to be immediately handled by all operators, addressed to J.C. Roth at Chicago, giving information as to the time the Zephyr passed Denver, Akron, McCook, Hastings, Lincoln, Pacific Junction, Creston, Osceola, Chariton, Albia, Ottumwa, Fairfield, Mt. Pleasant, Burlington, Monmouth, Galesburg, Kewanee, Princeton, Mendota, Aurora, Downers Grove, La Grange, Cicero, and Halsted Street Tower. Mr. Roth is to confer with Mr. McLaury and Mr. Worst and they, together, are to work out a plan of furnishing this information to some authorized person at A Century of Progress and also furnish it to any others who may desire it. After the trip of May 14 over the St. Charles Air Line, a close estimate will be furnished as to the length of time that will be required for movement of the Zephyr from St. Charles Air Line Junction to A Century of Progress.

Consider necessity of carrying an additional supply of water on the Zephyr; but before deciding this get information previously requested from the Budd Company about water capacity in various sections of the train.

Mr. Worst is to arrange with the Western Union Company so that they will render report as to the official leaving time at Denver, arriving time at Halsted Street, and arriving time at A Century of Progress.

Mr. Worst will report as quickly as possible to Mr. Gurley the exact arrangement which he has been able to make with the Western Union Company.

Mr. Worst is to immediately confer with Mr. Gardner and arrange to make installation of telephone instruments in

(a) enginemen's compartment convenient for use by the pilot who shall be seated behind the motorman,
(b) the "office desk" in the baggage compartment.

This should eliminate certain otherwise necessary trips through the Diesel engine compartment.

There are certain minor clearance restrictions which have been outlined in check made under Mr. Newton's guidance. It is understood that this information will be furnished to Superintendents and that these restrictions will be removed immediately. If it is not practicable to arrange clearance of Wharton derails according to standard height of 1 7/16", the Wharton derails will be removed for the day the Zephyr moves Denver to Chicago. It is very important that Superintendents check to be sure they get advice from Mr. Newton about these set clearances.

Any train orders which it may be necessary to deliver in emergency under the circumstances outlined on page 2 should be delivered as follows:

ON SINGLE TRACK, on station platform,
ON DOUBLE TRACK, on right hand side of train.

If it should be necessary to send messages to the Zephyr at any stations other than those we have enumerated, message should be sent to Mr. J.C. Roth, who will have other means of communicating with the Zephyr.

General Time Distribution Chart

Leave	Denver	4:00 A.M.	(Mountain Time)
Pass	Akron	5:20 A.M.	" "
Pass	McCook	7:00 A.M.	" "
Pass	McCook	8:00 A.M.	(Central Time)
Pass	Hastings, NE	9:40 A.M.	" "
Pass	Lincoln	10:50 A.M.	" "
Pass	Ashland	11:08 A.M.	" "
Pass	Oreapolis	11:40 A.M.	" "
Pass	Pacific Junction	11:50 A.M.	" "
Pass	Creston	12:50 P.M.	" "
Pass	Ottumwa	2:20 P.M.	" "
Pass	Galesburg	3:50 P.M.	" "
Enter	Airline Switch Chicago	6:00 P.M.	" "
Enter	A Century of Progress	6:30 P.M.	" "
Enter	A Century of Progress	7:30 P.M.	(Chicago Daylight Savings Time)

This was the scene at Denver Union Station moments before the start of the Denver to Chicago non-stop Pioneer Zephyr trip on May 26, 1934. Everything is primed and ready to go. Note the time on the Western Union clock mounted on the post at left.

Jack Ford's Mayfair Theatre Speech, New York City, January 15, 1935.

INTRODUCTION FOR JACK FORD

And now for a unique treat for the Mayfair fans. You are not going to meet a stunt artist, not an after dinner speaker, not a politician, not a movie star, but one of the world's greatest personalities in speed, engineer and master of the Burlington Zephyr Silver Streak train who has been at the throttle as she thundered night and day across the prairie and over dangerous mountain passes to write a new chapter in the annals of man's guidance of things mechanical hurtling through space.

Ladies and Gentlemen, meet a real friend for the great open spaces, a real man, a real hero of the modern iron horse, a man whose keen eye, steady hand, and courageous heart has for forty years brought millions of persons safely home across the roaring rails...Mr. Jack Ford, Engineer.

FORD'S SPEECH

This is my second most embarrassing moment. My first was when I received a Western Union telegram from Mr. Walter Reade, owner of this theatre, to come here and compete with Francis Lederer and Clark Gable. Me, who fired on the old hayburners back in the gay nineties when engine smokestacks and bustles were broad and high; and they've got May West across the street too. But I can safely put the Burlington Zephyr against May for platinum blondness, all around speed, fancy curves and detours, and general streamlining. And this Burlington baby is only a year old. You must come out to Kansas City or Omaha and see her sometime. Even though you can't accept this invitation, you are going to be riding before long on a powerful Diesel engine driven train, speedy, comfortable and safe. Two more are now being built for the Burlington Route. The Streak has been stepped up to 120 miles per hour. She holds the world's nonstop run for speed and distance between Denver and Chicago, 1,015 miles in the blinding time of 785 minutes, an average of 77.6 mph. She has been from Coast to Coast, and has asked no quarters from the Seaboard to the steepest grades in the Rockies. She has gone everywhere, calm and sure of herself, proudly pushing ahead like our old pioneers. I guess I have driven her about 50,000 miles since last April. Of course, I didn't know that they were taking her into Hollywood to be slicked up for the movies. But she stood the night life and the make-up better than I did. They left me out of the pictures, but I'm really hidden there in the engine, where there's always romance, thrills and drama. Like those real movie stars who were with me, you are going to get the ride of your life when you see her true to her name, graceful and beautiful, a shimmering streak cleaving the winds of Zephyrus. Unless they rush me back to the rails after this talk, I will be around the mezzanine, with the Zephyr model, and will be pleased to answer any questions about the most modern of trains.

Don't leave any "fan mail" for Engineer Jack Ford, but, leave it if you like for Miss Silver Streak.

Jack Ford's Mayfair Theatre, New York, appearance and speech. Walter Reade, owner of the Mayfair Theatre, New York, cleared Jack Ford's appearance and speech-making at the Mayfair with Ralph Budd. The purpose of Ford's appearance was opening night of the first showing of the RKO Radio Pictures Hollywood film called *Silver Streak*. Ford's speech was brief and was followed by a question and answer session on the mezzanine floor of the theater.

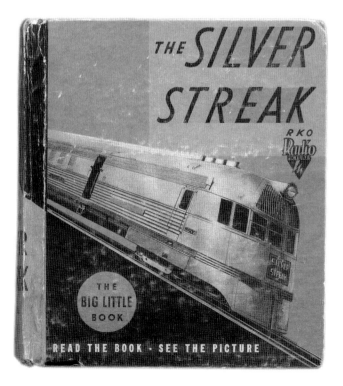

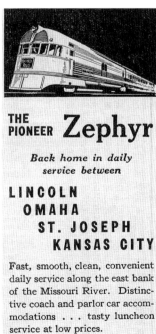

FAR LEFT. The Big Little book was a 4 x 4" children's book published to coincide with the *Silver Streak* movie. LEFT. The Burlington timetables promoted the Pioneer Zephyr and a "tasty luncheon service at low prices."

This oil painting, catching the spirit of "Zephyrus, the God of the West Wind," was later adopted as the Burlington's wall calendar for 1934. Note the children and the dog at left under the tree, and the state capitol building in Lincoln, Nebraska in the background.

Jack Ford: Every Boy's Hero!

Jack Ford was the man most associated with operating—the press of the day preferred the term "piloting"—the Zephyr. A career Burlington Route man, Ford hired on with the Burlington in the 1890's as a young fireman on the "spare board." Over the years he worked his way up the ladder, becoming a road foreman of engines on the Aurora Division in 1911 and assistant master mechanic in 1926.

Ralph Budd tapped the personable Ford to head the Zephyr introduction. Ford piloted the train on its first outing over the Reading on April 9, 1934 when it hit the impressive speed of 104 mph. He was at the throttle for a substantial amount of time during the speed run from Denver to Chicago on May 26, 1934 and remained with the train the majority of the time it was in exhibition service.

With smoking at the height of its popularity in the 1930's, it is not surprising that R. J Reynolds Tobacco arranged for print advertising featuring Jack Ford lighting up a Camel cigarette to "calm his nerves" after the record run.

When the Zephyr left the Century Exhibition and went west in its *Silver Streak* movie disguise, it was Jack Ford who made sure the silver screen star "hit its mark," as they still say in Hollywood and Broadway, every time on every cue.

Ford's involvement in the marketing of *Silver Streak* was limited to brief pre-screening remarks at its January 15, 1935 opening night at the Mayfair Theatre in New York City.

Three men responsible for the success of the Pioneer Zephyr were (left) Jack Ford, CB&O assistant master mechanic; (middle) Ernest Weber, CB&Q superintendent of automotive equipment; and Ernie Kuehn of General Motors' Electro-Motive Corp. They represented the new railroad technology age in their duster coats and overalls. The "W" on Kuehn's coveralls pocket was the logo of Winton Engine Corp., which supplied the diesel engine to EMC which installed it in the Zephyr. This was a composite photo of Ford, Weber, Kuehn, and the Zephyr—all combined in the darkroom.

Of more importance was Ford's use by Chicago toy train maker American Flyer Manufacturing Company to promote its O gauge copies of the new Zephyr. Jack Ford had become a true Hollywood hero to the impressionable boys of that more innocent age who crowded around him at every opportunity. Between December 13 and 23, 1934 Ford seemingly needed either a Zephyr or Santa's sleigh to get between department store Toylands from New York City to St. Louis! Jack Ford likely wanted only peace and quiet in a non-moving location by Christmas Day, 1934!

Jack Ford was once again in the media spotlight on October 23, 1936 when he piloted—with assistance—the new Denver Zephyr on its record-breaking Chicago-Denver "Gentlemen's Adventure" run which eclipsed the Pioneer Zephyr's dash by traveling between the two cities at an average speed of 83.33 mph.

After the promotion for the new Denver and Twin Cities Zephyrs died down, Jack Ford returned to the just "normally hectic" life of a road foreman of engines.

On May 26, 1960 Jack Ford once again sat at the throttle of the Pioneer Zephyr, but this time only for photos, as CB&Q #9900 joined him in retirement and was officially turned over to its new home and owner, Chicago's Museum of Science and Industry.

Railroading agreed with Jack Ford. He worked for the Burlington Route for more than 54 years and died at 91 years of age.

CHICAGO, BURLINGTON & QUINCY RAILROAD COMPANY
Passenger Department

Chicago, May 19, 1934.

TO AGENTS DENVER-CHICAGO MAIN LINE:

With the hope and expectation of enlisting the cooperation of the newspapers in the effort to guard against confusion and accident in connection with the fast non-stop run of the Zephyr from Denver to Chicago on the 26th, please deliver a copy of the following to each newspaper published in your city. An additional copy is enclosed for your bulletin board.

A. Cotsworth, Jr.
Passenger Traffic Manager.

- - - - - - - - - - -

TO EDITORS OF ALL NEWSPAPERS PUBLISHED AT
BURLINGTON MAIN LINE POINTS DENVER TO CHICAGO:

You have doubtless heard that on Saturday, May 26th, the Burlington's new Diesel-powered, stainless steel, streamline train, the Zephyr, will make a high-speed, non-stop run from Denver to Chicago, starting in the early morning and terminating that evening at the Century of Progress grounds, as a part of the ceremonies incident to the opening of the Fair on that date.

While every conceivable precaution in the interest of safety is being taken, we are dependent to a considerable extent upon the cooperation of the citizens of the communities through which the train will pass. If this distance of something over a thousand miles is to be covered between dawn and dusk, a high rate of speed will be necessary through the various intermediate cities and towns, and to insure against confusion or accidents, it is highly important that all of those who are interested in watching the progress of the Zephyr through their community stand well back from the track. At stations, they should not be closer than the back line of the station platform, and at other places back of the outer line of the right-of-way. Where people may gather on bridges to watch the Zephyr pass below them, it is also important that nothing be dropped on the track ahead of it nor on the train as it passes.

We are anxious that nothing within reason be left undone to insure the success of this enterprise, and in the interest of the safety of onlookers as well as those on board the train, it seems appropriate to address this letter to the editors of all newspapers published at the various cities and towns through which the Zephyr will pass to ask that they impress upon their readers the importance of carefully observing the suggestions contained herein.

Your cooperation in the matter will be greatly appreciated.

A. Cotsworth, Jr.
Passenger Traffic Manager
Burlington Route.

This May 19, 1934 press release was issued to all Burlington Railroad agents between Chicago and Denver, asking them to deliver a copy of the release to all newspapers in their territory. The railroad was concerned that accidents during the non-stop trip would mar the otherwise festive atmosphere and goodwill created by the train. *Museum of Science and Industry archives*

From its christening on April 18, 1934 through the fall of that year, the Pioneer Zephyr traveled 30,437 miles, visited 222 cities and towns and was inspected by more than 2 million people.

Burlington

THE WEST WIND

Zephyr

and Presents America's ➡ First Diesel Streamline Train

Wings to the Iron Horse

The Zephyr

BURLINGTON'S STREAMLINE MOTOR TRAIN

Built of stainless steel.

Powered by an eight cylinder two-cycle 660 H.P., oil-burning Diesel engine.

Rides on articulated trucks.

Runs on roller bearings.

Air-conditioned in all passenger compartments.

Equipped for radio reception.

Windows of shatter-proof glass.

Electro-pneumatic brakes.

It is 197 feet long—Carries 72 passengers.

After making a coast-to-coast tour, the train will be on exhibition at A Century of Progress Exposition in Chicago.

Burlington Pioneers Again ➡ In Gleaming Stainless Steel ➡

The reclining chairs in the smoking room are done in fine leather in harmony with the soft tans of walls and ceiling.

The flashing outside surface of the train is unpainted; the inside sills and ornamental moulding likewise remain in their natural bright finish.

The ingenious electric buffet-grill is a masterpiece in compactness and efficiency.

Adjustable chairs in duo-tone shades of pearl-green, glass curtains to match, a rich rug to soften it; foot-fall—the 40-passenger compartment is modern as the moment.

The mountain comes to Mahomet, as meals from the grill are served upon tables set up at your chair.

A keen little solarium fitted with detached chairs occupies the glass-enclosed rear of the last car.

The ZEPHYR . . . new revolutionary type of streamline motor train presented by the Chicago, Burlington & Quincy Railroad, is a three-car all-metal assembly, much lighter in weight than the usual type of train. It is novel in design; unique in the application of automotive principles new to rail travel; and basically different from conventional trains in structural composition.

The ZEPHYR is 197 feet in length; has seats for 72 passengers, and is designed for day-time travel.

Not only as to exterior sheathing and interior finishing, but as to framework as well, it is built of stainless steel—a modern non-corrosive alloy consisting of 18 per cent chromium and 8 per cent nickel, cold-rolled, and characterized by its great ruggedness, ductility, and high tensile strength.

Practically every plate, sheet, strut, beam or other part is secured by means of electric welding rather than riveting. This welding takes advantage of the new Budd "shot-weld" process in which each "shot" of electricity is precisely timed, resulting in absolute uniformity in welds which occur as close together as the stitches in a seam; unifying the sections effectually and without breakdown of the molecular qualities of the metal.

New sources of power, new methods of transmission were sought.

The first of a heralded new type of two-cycle, oil-burning Diesel engine, developed especially for the ZEPHYR by the Winton division of General Motors, furnishes its motive power. Without spark plugs or ignition system of the sort used in gas engines, combustion is accomplished wholly through compression.

The ZEPHYR has only sixteen wheels altogether (a train having three cars of conventional equipment would have thirty-six) the rear of one car and the front of the succeeding one resting upon the same truck—the heralded articulated method which makes for economy, light weight, smooth riding qualities, less noise; and

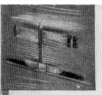

eliminates "slack" between the cars. Trucks are rubber-cushioned at points of impact. Wheels are solid steel alloy with integral tread, rim-toughened to render long service without regrinding or replacement.

The first unit is occupied by the engine room and a large compartment for the handling of U. S. Mail. The second unit provides space for baggage and express, an ingenious buffet-grill and smoking compartment. The front half of the third unit is devoted to reclining chairs, while the rear part is an extraordinary little lounge room which conforms to the bullet-shaped end of the train.

A real solarium with wide, curved glass windows all around to afford a 180-degree field of vision; equipped with detached easy chairs, it offers luxurious accommodations equal to the highest class of parlor car service.

Meals from the buffet-grill are served upon tables set up for the occasion at your chair.

Pat. No. 1,955,117. Ebersold-Oliver, Inc., Chicago

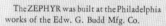

The train weighs approximately 95 tons, or about as much as one Pullman car, and is capable of a speed exceeding 100 miles an hour.

Trim as a sail-boat; speed king of the rails—the ZEPHYR strikes the most advanced note in up-to-date transport methods, and writes a colorful, interesting and significant chapter into American railroad history.

The ZEPHYR was built at the Philadelphia works of the Edw. G. Budd Mfg. Co.

Mr. Paul Cret of Philadelphia was consulting architect for the builders in charge of the interior decorative treatment.

The Chicago builders, Holabird & Root, were consulting architects for the Burlington in the train's styling.

Burlington Route

PRESENTED BY
CHICAGO, BURLINGTON & QUINCY RAILROAD

Part of a Burlington Railroad promotional brochure, this colorful paper publicity generated ample traffic for the new Zephyr, as well as those many Zephyrs that followed.

This is one of the many Burlington Railroad postcards that circulated when the Zephyrs were in service. The postcards helped lend an air of prestige to traveling by train. *Don Heimburger collection*

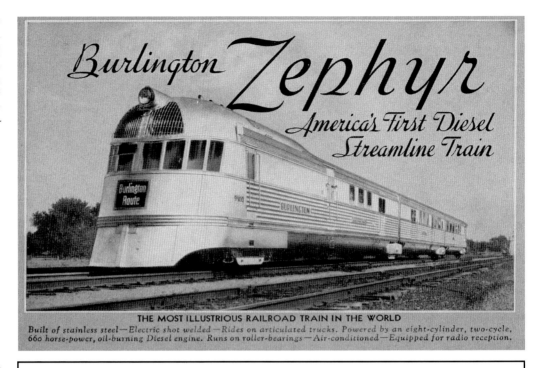

THE MOST ILLUSTRIOUS RAILROAD TRAIN IN THE WORLD
Built of stainless steel—Electric shot welded—Rides on articulated trucks. Powered by an eight-cylinder, two-cycle, 660 horse-power, oil-burning Diesel engine. Runs on roller-bearings—Air-conditioned—Equipped for radio reception.

This list captures some of the highlights of the Pioneer Zephyr between June of 1933 and July of 1998, including the restored Zephyr being returned to the Museum of Science and Industry in Chicago and put on display there in the Great Hall.

Pioneer Zephyr Milestones

June 17, 1933	Zephyr ordered by CB&Q RR
Apr. 7, 1934	Zephyr completed
Apr. 9, 1934	Zephyr test run–top speed 104 mph
Apr. 18, 1934	Zephyr christened
May 26, 1934	Nonstop Dawn-Dusk Run from Denver-Chicago
Sept., 1934	Filmed for motion picture, "Silver Streak"
Nov. 11, 1934	Zephyr put into service
Nov. 11, 1934–April 27, 1936	Lincoln, NE-Omaha, NE-Kansas City, MO route
June 24, 1935	4th car added
May, 1936	New diesel engine installed
May 31, 1936–Nov. 8, 1936	Chicago, IL - Denver, CO route as Advance Denver Zephyr
Nov. 11, 1936	Train renamed Pioneer Zephyr
Nov. 11, 1936–Oct. 23, 1938	Lincoln, NE-Omaha, NE-Kansas City, MO route
Oct. 24, 1938–April 29, 1939	St. Louis-Kansas City, MO route
May 2, 1939–Oct. 2, 1939	Lincoln, NE-Omaha, NE-Kansas City, MO route
Oct. 2, 1939	Head-on collision with freight train
Dec. 6, 1939–Mar. 13, 1940	Lincoln, NE-Omaha, NE-Kansas City, MO route
December 29, 1939	Passed million-mile service mark
Mar. 14–23, 1940	Ft. Worth-Houston, TX route
Mar. 24–Apr. 14, 1940	Lincoln, NE-Omaha, NE-Kansas City, MO route
Apr. 15–29, 1940	St. Louis-Kansas City, MO route
Apr. 30, 1940–Jan. 31, 1942	St. Louis, MO-Burlington, IA route
Feb. 1–Mar. 7, 1942	Toured Nebraska selling war bonds
Mar. 8, 1942–June 30, 1948	Lincoln-McCook, NE route
Apr. 10, 1944	Celebrated 10th birthday
Nov. 12, 1944	Rear car struck by freight train
July 1-Oct. 4, 1948	At Chicago Railroad Fair
Nov. 14, 1948–Apr. 29, 1949	Ft. Worth-Houston, TX route
Apr. 29, 1949	Hit concrete truck at Houston
Aug. 27–Sept. 30, 1949	At Chicago Railroad Fair
Oct. 15, 1949–Apr. 29, 1950	Denver, CO-Cheyenne, WY route
Apr. 29, 1950	Hit truck at Longmont, CO
May, 1950	4th car removed
Oct. 18, 1950–Jan. 31, 1953	Galesburg-Quincy, IL route
Feb. 1, 1953–Mar. 16, 1957	Galesburg, IL-Quincy, IL-St. Joseph, MO route
Mar. 17–Aug. 2 1957	Quincy, IL-St. Joseph, MO route
Aug. 3, 1957–Feb. 20, 1960	St. Joseph, MO-Lincoln, NE route
Feb. 20, 1960	Final day in revenue service
Mar. 20, 1960	Final run from Lincoln, NE to Galesburg, IL
May 26, 1960	Presented to Museum of Science and Industry
June 30, 1964	Original diesel engine donated to Smithsonian
Oct., 1997	Restored Pioneer Zephyr installed in Great Hall
July 16, 1998	Restored Pioneer Zephyr opened for display in Great Hall

An airplane follows the three-car Pioneer Zephyr near Bristol, Illinois on its trip from Denver to Chicago. The trip caused great excitement, as well as a couple of anxious moments for the crew when some cables overheated and the air brake pressure dropped.

PIONEER ZEPHYR
Completely Air-Conditioned
No Extra Fare

NORTHBOUND—No. 21
Solarium-Parlor Lounge
Kansas City to Omaha-Lincoln
Coaches—Kansas City to Omaha-Lincoln
Buffet-Grill Service—For all meals

NORTHBOUND—No. 23
Sleeping Cars A C
Kansas City to Omaha—D.R., Sections
(May be occupied until 8.00 a.m.)
Kansas City to Lincoln via Omaha—
D.R., Sections (Ready at Kansas City
10.00 p.m.)
Chair Car A C—Kansas City to Omaha
and Lincoln

NORTHBOUND—No. 27
Dining-Parlor Car A C
Kansas City to Omaha
Coach A C—Kansas City to Omaha

SOUTHBOUND—No. 20
Solarium-Parlor-Lounge
Lincoln-Omaha to Kansas City
Coaches—Lincoln-Omaha to Kansas City
Buffet-Grill Service—For all meals

SOUTHBOUND—No. 22
Sleeping Cars A C
Lincoln and Omaha to Kansas City—
D.R., Sections (Ready at Lincoln and
Omaha 9.30 p.m.)
Chair Car A C
Omaha to Kansas City
Coach
Lincoln to Omaha

SOUTHBOUND—No. 26
Dining-Parlor Car A C
Omaha to Kansas City
Coach A C—Omaha to Kansas City

NORTHBOUND—No. 302-41
Observation-Sleeping Car A C
Denver to Billings—Sections
Observation-Parlor Car
Edgemont to Deadwood
Sleeping Cars A C
Alliance to Billings—D.R., Sections
Dining Car—Alliance to Sheridan
Chair Car—Denver to Alliance-Billings

SOUTHBOUND—No. 42-301
Observation Sleeping Car A C
Billings to Denver—Sections
Observation-Parlor Car
Deadwood to Edgemont
Sleeping Cars A C
Tacoma-Billings-Alliance (Table F)
D.R., Compt., Sections
Dining Car A C
Billings to Alliance
Chair Car
Billings to Alliance-Denver

NORTHBOUND—No. 304-43
Sleeping Cars A C
Alliance to Billings and Tacoma (Table F)
D.R., Compt., Sections
Dining Car A C—Alliance to Billings
Chair Car A C—Alliance to Billings
Coach—Denver to Alliance

SOUTHBOUND—No. 44-303
Sleeping Cars A C
Billings-Alliance—D. R., Sections
Dining Car—Sheridan to Alliance
Chair Car
Billings to Alliance
Alliance to Denver

NORTHBOUND—No. 29
Observation-Sleeping Car A C
Denver to Billings—Sections
Sleeping Car
Cheyenne to Casper—D. R., Sections
(ready at 9.30 p.m.; set at Casper
until 8.00 a.m.)
Dining Car A C—Casper to Basin
Coach A C—Denver to Billings

SOUTHBOUND—No. 30
Observation-Sleeping Car A C
Billings to Denver
Sections
Sleeping Car
Casper to Cheyenne—D.R., Sections
(Set at Cheyenne until 8.00 a.m.)
Dining Car A C—Basin to Casper
Coach A C—Billings to Denver

ZEPHYR CONNECTION

NORTHBOUND—No. 31
Observation-Coach
Buffet Service

SOUTHBOUND—No. 32
Observation-Coach
Buffet Service

Reference Marks
‖ Meals. ⊙ Connection. ‡ Motor Car. § Via Hannibal. f Flag stop. † Daily except
Sunday. ◆ Burlington bus between Cody and Deaver connects with Trains 29 and 30
to and from Billings.
A C—Regularly assigned cars Air-Conditioned

Burlington Zephyr Time Table, December, 1936 - January, 1937

LEFT. The Burlington highlighted Zephyr playing cards in their timetables. A single deck cost only $.40.

This photo was taken from an overhead plane near Otis, Colorado as the Pioneer Zephyr made its record-breaking run in 1934 between Denver and Chicago. The train rolled into the Windy City that evening, after departing Denver at 5:04:40 a.m.

ZEPHYR 9900

Purchased from Edw. G. Budd Company on AFE 28022, cost $208,561.88.

Three car stainless steel, streamlined train, Diesel Locomotive, 600 HP, 8 cylinder, 2 cycle.

Passenger capacity: 52 coach
                     12 parlor
                      8 dinnette - used for meal service as well as
                     —— for accommodation of short haul passengers.
                     72

4-9-34 - Made first run, Philadelphia to Perkiomem Jot and return.

4-17-34- Turned over to CB&Q at Philadelphia.

4-18-34 to 5-10-34 - Toured east - visited 30 cities and towns, made 2900 miles and had 379,857 visitors.

5-11-34 and 5-12-34 - Exhibited at Chicago - 33,565 visitors.

5-13-34 to 5-17-34 - West Burlington shop for general inspection.

5-18-34 to 5-24-34 - Exhibited along line Burlington to Denver - Visited 16 cities and towns, 824 miles and had 105040 visitors.

5-25-34 - At Denver shop.

5-26-34 - Made record non-stop run Denver to Chicago in 13 hours and 5 minutes at an average speed of 77.6 miles per hour. Had total of 82 people on train, 48 being Burlington representatives, 20 press representatives, etc.

5-27-34 - Exhibited at "A Century of Progress" - 15,757 visitors.

5-28-34 - Chicago-Aurora excursion trips - 950 people.

5-29-34 to 6-8-34 - Toured 36 midwest cities and towns - 1609 miles, 171724 visitors.

6-9-34 and 6-10-34 - West Burlington shop for inspection.

6-11-34 and 6-12-34 - Exhibited St.Joseph,Atchison,Leavenworth and Kansas City - 363 miles - 39,886 visitors.

6-13-34 - Omaha Chamber of Commerce Good Will Tour to Hastings.

6-14-34 - Lincoln Chamber of Commerce to Holdredge,Nebr.

A West Burlington, Iowa farmer in his field—along with 1.5 million others—got a glimpse of the Zephyr as it rolled east toward Chicago under fair skies. Three teams of men operated the train on its epic 1934 journey.

-2-

6-15-34 - Enroute Denver.

6-16-34 - Left Denver 6.30 AM for Pacific Coast Tour.

6-16-34 to 6-28-34 - Toured Pacific Coast cities and towns - 30 cities and towns - 4217 miles - 172,134 visitors.

6-29-34 - Inspection by American Society of Mechanical Engineers.

6-30-34 to 7-9-34 - Lines West Tour - Visited 62 cities and towns - 2769 miles - 147216 visitors.

7-10-34 to 7-13-34 - West Burlington shop for general inspection.

7-14-34 to 7-29-34 - At "A Century of Progress" - 708,964 visitors.

7-30-34 and 7-31-34 - Test run Chicago to Minneapolis and return - Northbound trip made in 363 minutes or average speed of 71.01 miles per hour and southbound trip made in 269 minutes - six intermediate stops being made in each direction.

8-1-34 to 8-19-34 - At "A Century of Progress".

8-20-34 - Test run Chicago to Flag Center and return.

8-21-34 to 9-3-34 - At "A Century of Progress".

9-4-34 to 9-5-34 - Nebraska State Fair - Lincoln.

9-6-34 and 9-7-34 - At "A Century of Progress".

9-8-34 to 10-4-34 - To Pacific Coast and return, to film the picture "The Silver Streak".

10-5-34 - Enroute Los Angeles to Amarillo, Texas.

10-6-34 to 10-16-34 - Exhibited in Texas and Oklahoma - 19 cities and towns, 3396 miles, 193,700 visitors.

10-17-34 - Enroute West Burlington shop.

10-18-34 and 10-19-34 - At West Burlington shop fixing train up for brake tests between Aurora and Zearing.

10-20-34 to 10-31-34 - Making brake tests between Aurora and Zearing.

This typewritten memorandum was written by the Burlington Railroad, establishing important dates in the life of the Pioneer Zephyr between the years 1934 and 1938. With so much fanfare about the train, it's odd to see that the Zephyr remained idle on November 6, 1934. *Museum of Science and Industry archives*

-3-

11-1-34 - Exhibited Hannibal and Brookfield Divisions - 8 cities and towns, 430 miles - 14,439 visitors.

11-2-34 - St.Joseph Chamber of Commerce trips.

Up to this time had visited 192 cities Chicago and west, having 1,656,749 visitors and total of 222 cities in US or total of 2,016,606 visitors.

11-3-34 to 11-5-34 - Introductory excursions between Lincoln.Omaha and Pacific Junction.

11-6-34 - Idle

11-7-34 to 11-10-34 - Round trips St.Joseph and Kansas City.

11-11-34 - Inaugural Trip - Trains 20 and 21 between Lincoln and Kansas City.

Up to this point, have shown daily movements. From here on will show only the changes in service or changes made in train.

6-24-35 - A fourth car - 40 seat coach - added.

4-26-36 to 5-26-36 - In Aurora shop amplifying air conditioning system. Diesel motor that came with train, was removed and new one installed. The 40 seat coach was removed from train at this time and was used in 9902.

5-31-36 - Established "Advance Denver Zephyr".

11-7-36 - Withdrawn from Chicago-Denver service at Omaha.

11-9-36 - Added baggage car "Becky Thatcher" at Havelock shop. This car had been removed from Zephyr 9903.

11-11-36 - Replaced in Lincoln-Kansas City run.

12-26-36 - Baggage car "Becky Thatcher" removed.

1-30-37 - A fourth car added. This was the 40 coach seat car that had been removed in May, 1936 and used on 9902. Was added at Lincoln.

6-27-38 - Fourth car removed and sent to Texas for Zephyr 9901. This was the 40 coach seat car.

6-28-38 - New dinnette-coach added. (#500)

10-24-38 - Assigned to trains 32-33 between Kansas City and St. Louis.

This crystal clear photograph was taken at the Wings of a Century Pageant, part of the 1934 World's Fair held on Chicago's lakefront, following the Zephyr's historic May 26 Denver to Chicago journey.

Zephyr 9900

Received from builders - 4-17-34 at Philadelphia.

Placed in service - 11-11-34 between Lincoln and Kansas City.

Was three car unit when received - consisting of power unit and two cars.

Fourth car placed in train 6-24-35. This was purchased on AFE 28151 at cost of $48,000.00 (AFE shows $48,000.00 but actual cost was $53,156.89)

The fourth car purchased on AFE 28151, was removed and Dinette coach 500, purchased on AFE 28533 (This AFE covered several stainless steel cars from Edw. G. Budd Company) at cost of $82,661.37, was placed in train on June 28, 1938 at Havelock. The car removed, was loaded on flat car and sent to Texas for application to Zephyr 9901.

Traction motors 1648957 and 1648958 were received with Zephyr 9900 from the Budd Company.

On April 8th, 1937, Executive Vice President's office issued statement on comparison of the Zephyr trains and following is information for Zephyr 9900:

Engine Horsepower (Propulsion)	600
Total weight of train	284,918#
Weight per Horsepower	474.86#
Pounds Trailing Load (per horsepower) --	307.34#
Weight on power wheels	100,515#
Weight on trailing wheels	184,403#
Number of power axles	2
Number of power trucks	1
Number of cars, including power	4
Number trailer cars	About 2-1/2

Weight on Rail - Ready to run	
Truck No. 1	100,515#
Truck No. 2	56,695#
Truck No. 3	52,324#
Truck No. 4	44,824#
Truck No. 5	30,560#
Total	284,918#

On February 11th, 1938, Executive Vice President's office made up statement, showing tractive effort rating on Zephyrs, and following is information for Zephyr 9900:

Speed	Tractive Effort
Start (Max.) ---	23,860 lbs.
10	13,500 "
20	8,200 "
30	5,850 "
40	4,500 "
50	3,625 "
60	3,000 "
70	2,550 "
80	2,150 "
90	1,850 "
95	1,750 "
100	1,600 "

Zephyr 9900 is known as Model 8-201-A - 8 cylinder - 2 cycle - solid injection uniflow scavenging Diesel engine.

The eight cylinders develop 75 HP each or 600 HP, at 750 RPM.

On 6-10-38 Mr. C.F.Zaitz of Electro-Motive Corporation worked up "Engineering Data On Winton Diesel Engines" and information on 8-201-A engine, is as follows:

Number of cylinders	8
Bore	8"
Stroke	10"
Stroke - bore ratio	1.25
Area of one piston	50.265 Sq.In.
Displacement of one piston	502.65 cu.in.
Total displacement volume	4021.2 cu.in.
Volume compression space (1 cyl)	33.51 cu.in.
Compression ratio (Approx.)	16.1
Normal brake horsepower	600
Normal speed - R.P.M.	750
Normal piston speed	1250 Ft./min.
Brake mean effective pressure	79 P.S.I.
Torque	4201 Ft.Lbs.
Displacement per horsepower	6.70 cu.in.
Valve dia. - exhaust	2-3/4
Valve lift	.571"
Valve area	3.7 sq.in.

ABOVE. An artist took the photograph on the previous page and highlighted it by airbrushing, altered the "Burlington Route" herald on the front to be more recognizable and made the headlight "glow."

When the Pioneer Zephyr reached Chicago's Union Station on May 26, these "Zephyr Dawn to Dusk Club" members were photographed, along with Zeph, the "Zephyr mascot." Albert Cotsworth, Jr., Burlington's passenger traffic manager, holds the reins to the donkey, which was presented by the Rocky Mountain News to the Century of Progress Exposition.

ABOVE AND NEXT PAGE TOP RIGHT. After another tour of the far West and South, the Zephyr returned to the World's Fair in Chicago and was on exhibit between July 14 to September 2, 1934. Long lines of people waited to tour the Zephyr's three stainless steel cars. To the left of the Zephyr (next page) is Burlington's woodburner No. 35, a 4-4-0 with a balloon stack.

RIGHT. In small towns and large cities alike, the Pioneer Zephyr was received with great enthusiasm, with hundreds turning out to see the fastest train in the world. Location is Exhibition Avenue, Los Angeles, June, 1934. FAR RIGHT. This photo was taken at a small Colorado town in June of 1934 where the Zephyr was exhibited.

The Zephyr leads a procession of three Denver & Rio Grande Western Railroad trains westbound through the six-mile Moffat Tunnel, thus becoming the first train through the new Denver to Salt Lake City shortcut on June 16, 1934.

Gliding smoothly over a bridge near San Francisco, the Zephyr displays its sleek design and modernistic features during its June, 1934 West Coast tour.

Throughout the Zephyr's publicity tour, the 600 hp oil-burning diesel engine, riding on articulated trucks, powered the train through many of America's most well-known landmarks such as Colorado's Royal Gorge.

At Orestod (Bond), Colorado on June 16, 1939, the 197-foot-long Zephyr was the backdrop for the Denver & Rio Grande's Western's Dotsero Cutoff opening Silver Spike festivities. The Zephyr sits on the Cutoff trackage, ready to complete its trip to Oakland, having just passed over the new line.

Pioneer Zephyr Menu, 1934

Breakfast

Tomato, Prune, Pineapple or Orange Juice	20¢
Grapefruit, Half	20¢
Orange, Whole or Sliced	10¢
Dry Cereal with Cream	25¢
Eggs–Fried or Scrambled	25¢
Dry or Buttered Toast with Jelly/Marmalade	10¢
Sweet Roll or 2 Doughnuts	10¢
Coffee (cup)	10¢
Individual Bottle of Milk	10¢
Coffee or Cocoa (pot)	20¢

Lunch/Dinner

Ham/Cheese Sandwich	20¢
Hamburger	20¢
Hot Dog	20¢
Fried Egg Sandwich	20¢
Baked Beans, Hot/Cold with Brown Bread	30¢
Spaghetti with Tomato Sauce	25¢
Lettuce-Tomato Salad	25¢
Fruit or Shrimp Salad	35¢
Bread & Butter or Toast	10¢
Strawberry Preserves	20¢
Grapefruit, Half	20¢

Individual Pie	10¢
Ice Cream with Cookies	25¢
Individual Bottle Milk	10¢
Coffee, Tea, Cocoa (pot)	20¢
Coffee, cup	10¢
Lemonade	Glass
Orangeade	Glass
Ginger Ale	Split 15¢ Pint 25¢
Apollinaris Water 3 oz. 10¢ Split 20¢ Pint 30¢	
White Rock Lithia Water Split 20¢ Pint 30¢	
Ale	Bottle 25¢
Beer	Bottle 25¢
Whiskey	Individual 25¢, 40¢, 50¢
Brandy	Individual 50¢
Gin	Individual 25¢
Cocktail	Individual 35¢
Cigars	5¢, 10¢, 15¢, 2 for 25¢
Cigarettes	15¢ & 25¢ (Not sold in Iowa)
Playing Cards	Pack 40¢
Bromo Seltzer	Individual 15¢
Aspirin	Box 12 25¢

This oil painting shows the Pioneer Zephyr, on its Western cities tour in June of 1934, heading over the Dotsero Cutoff. The stainless steel train was barnstorming over the country, making friends and headlines everywhere it went.

See the Burlington's "ZEPHYR"

The STREAMLINED "STAR" of the thrilling railroad drama

the SILVER STREAK

Burlington Route

SOON TO BE SHOWN
AT LEADING THEATRES

One of the outstanding photo-plays of the day, it enriches our fictional Americana with a new and stirring Romance of the Rails.

If you saw the famous streamline ZEPHYR on its coast-to-coast tour, or on exhibition at A Century of Progress Exposition; or on its world-record, non-stop dash from Denver to Chicago, you will thrill anew at the sight of the bullet train speeding through the title role of this distinctly new type of film feature.

If you haven't seen the ZEPHYR, here is an opportunity to view the wonder-train at close range as it flashes through a streamline saga of straining steel and grinding wheels . . . . . a new-style Iron Horse hurtling across the Western plains and rushing headlong through the mountains in an exciting race against time.

RKO-RADIO
PICTURE with
SALLY BLANE
CHARLES STARRETT
HARDIE ALBRIGHT
WILLIAM FARNUM
DIRECTED BY THOMAS ATKINS

ALL PHOTOS. "One of the outstanding photo-plays of the day, it enriches our fictional Americana with a new and stirring Romance of the Rails," says the promotional advertisement for the *Silver Streak* movie, based on the Pioneer Zephyr. Under the direction of Thomas Atkins, the RKO Studios motion picture entitled *Silver Streak* was produced by Glendon Allvine, once a railroad man himself. Starring in the picture was Sally Blane, Charles Starrett, Hardie Albright and William Farnum. In the movie, the *Silver Streak* was the design of a young engineer who wins acceptance by the president of the C.B. & D. Railroad only with the greatest of difficulty. The 72-minute film cost $122,000 to make and was photographed on the Burlington, Rio Grande and Union Pacific railroads between September 7 and October 2, 1934. The advertisement calls the Zephyr "the wonder-train."

Chapter 6

— Zephyr's 25½ Years —
in the Work-a-Day World

On November 11, 1934, Armistice Day to that generation of Americans, the Burlington Zephyr entered service between Lincoln, Nebraska and Kansas City, Missouri via Omaha. That morning a large crowd was in attendance as Nebraska Governor Charles W. Bryan offered remarks and shook Motorman Jack Ford's hand for the cameras.

Since the Union Pacific's M-10000 was still in exhibition service when the Zephyr departed Lincoln that morning, #9900 entered the history books as the first streamlined and first diesel-electric-powered passenger train placed in service in North America.

The Zephyr made a daily 500-mile roundtrip, departing Lincoln as CB&Q Train #20 at 7:30 a.m., and arriving at Omaha—55 miles distant—at 8:25 a.m.. After a 35-minute Omaha station stop the streamliner continued 195 miles to Kansas City, arriving at 1:00 p.m. The return trip left Kansas City as CB&Q Train #21 at 2:30 p.m and arrived at Omaha at 6:30 p.m. It left Omaha at 7:00 p.m and arrived at Lincoln at 7:55 p.m.

Maintenance and other servicing was initially done overnight at an open pit under an open-sided shed in Lincoln. Initially assigned to the work was one machinist, one electrician, two outside car cleaners, two inside car cleaners and one car inspector. Since several gas-electric cars were based in Lincoln, the local motor car maintainer could be called in on an emergency basis if necessary.

The entire train's exterior was washed nightly with Bonami brand cleanser.

The three-car 108-ton fully-provisioned Zephyr replaced a steam-powered local of five or six cars weighing between 314 and 404.5 total tons.

ALWAYS SOLD OUT

The 72-seat train was immediately and consistently sold out—frequently for days in advance—in both directions, this in spite of the fact that just days before entering service the Zephyr had run numerous excursions during early November out of Lincoln, Omaha, St. Joseph, Weston, Atchison, Leavenworth and Kansas City to satisfy a curious and fascinated public. People gladly parted with $0.75 to $1.25 for a 60-to-90 minute roundtrip on the Zephyr. It was proof a better tomorrow was at hand.

In response to the overwhelming popularity of its new stream-line train (the term "streamliner" having not yet entered the lexicon), the Burlington Route promptly is-

sued AFE #28151 to Budd for one new 40-seat stainless steel coach to expand #9900 to four cars and 112 seats. Even in the Depression inflation was not unknown, as the original purchase order authorization was for $48,000.00. Chair car #525's final cost was recorded as $53,156.89, a significant 10.74% increase.

AVERAGE 97% AVAILABILITY

During the Burlington Zephyr's first year of service it averaged 97% availability (354 out of 365 days) and carried an average of 204 passengers per day, an increase of 50% over the prior year. Whereas during December 1934 and January 1935, overall "Q" passenger patronage increased 26% over the previous year, little #9900's patronage increased a whopping 196%! Equally impressive was the streamline train's operating expense of but $0.35 per train mile, only 60% of the $0.59 per train mile cost of the steam train it replaced. The Zephyr lowered costs while increasing revenue and passenger loads. Railroad executives across America took notice.

On June 24, 1935 the Zephyr was removed from service just long enough to have freshly delivered all-chair car #525 added to its articulated consist. The now four-car train seated 112 passengers.

Upon completion of its April 27, 1936 run the Zephyr was removed from its Lincoln-Omaha-Kansas City assignment and had chair car #525 removed, and a new Winton engine installed. Spiffed up and reassembled, #9900 joined similarly reassigned three-car Twin Cities Zephyr #9903 to provide daily service as Trains #1 and #10 between Chicago and Denver as the Advance Denver Zephyr on a 16-hour overnight schedule. The coach-buffet streamline trains were a "holding action" to protect the "Q's" reputation, and mail contract, against the new Union Pacific 10-car City of Denver articulated trainsets placed in service on June 18, 1936.

ADVANCE ZEPHYR

The Advance Denver Zephyr service operated between May 31 and November 8, 1936.

Zephyr #9900 made a total of 161 trips of 1,034 miles each and had a 98.1% on-time record. The schedule required the train to average 65 miles per hour during each trip.

On November 11, 1936 CB&Q #9900 was guest of honor at its second birthday party. The train was formally renamed the Pioneer Zephyr with new nameplates so stating attached to each side of the observation lounge. Beginning that day #9900 returned to its original Lincoln-Omaha-Kansas City

The record-breaking Pioneer Zephyr glides into Chicago's Union Station in 1934. You can see the motorman through the window at left.

A firsthand Zephyr report

About a month after going into service, #9900 had a very interested but otherwise unremarked passenger named Ernest K. Bloss aboard. Bloss was—to quote his business card—Supervisor of Motor Cars, Mechanical Department, Boston & Maine Railroad, Boston, Mass.

What few of Bloss' fellow passengers knew, as he chatted with them, sampled the Zephyr's buffet cuisine, and rode in both coach and observation lounge, was that the Budd Company had nearly completed its second diesel-electric powered stainless steel articulated streamliner, and it was not for the Burlington Route.

B&M management had sent Ernie "out West" to get what today we'd call feedback from the "Q's" paying passengers and operating crew. His favorable first person report to B&MRR Chief Mechanical Officer D. C. Reid was filed the day after Christmas, 1934, and gives an unusually intimate view of the earliest days of Zephyr operation.

Streamline Train - Zephyr Operation

Mr. Reid:

The following are my comments on the operation of the Burlington Zephyr.

I rode this train from Omaha to Kansas City and return and then from Omaha to Lincoln. The first part of this run from Omaha to Kansas City is 195 miles and is made in four hours with 10 to 12 stops. This gives an average distance between stops of about 20 miles and a scheduled speed of 49 miles per hour. The top speed attained to do this is 85 miles an hour.

The run between Omaha and Lincoln is a non-stop run of 55 miles and is made in 55 minutes. On both runs there are several slow-downs, quite a bit of territory where the speed is restricted to 60 miles per hour and it is necessary to maintain the top speed of 80 to 85 miles an hour over a considerable portion of the run in order to make the schedule.

Between Omaha and Kansas City I rode the observation car and other passenger space. The riding qualities in the passenger compartment are very good and the riding qualities in the observation compartment are very much better than they were when the train was East. There is, however, still room for improvement and the Burlington are (sic) changing the shock absorber system on the last truck this week. The up and down riding qualities are extremely good but the difficulty seems to be with the side sway or 'whit' action of the rear truck. In view of the improvement that has been made, I feel eventually this problem can be worked out satisfactorily.

This train, formerly handling about 25 or 30 passengers, is now handling capacity load (74*) and is turning away so much business that it is necessary to run a second section. This second section is a steam train and is operated as closely as possible to the Zephyr's schedule and is having a very bad effect on the track conditions.

On account of the fact that they are handling 100% capacity load, they are somewhat embarrassed by lack of proper baggage facilities. As you know, our train is arranged with baggage racks in each car but the "Zephyr" had baggage racks for the observation compartment only. All of the baggage for the smoker and passenger compartment is carried in the baggage room and uses up about 15 feet of baggage room space along one side of the car. Burlington intends to install steel baggage racks for the convenient handling of this baggage sometime this week.

I made use of the buffet service and was very much pleased with this. The prices are very reasonable and the portions are generous and the service good. The public reaction to this service is extremely good, judging by the comments I heard from all those who used the buffet service.

Operation

This train is operated over the usual mid-western road conditions, being about 100# (pounds-to-the-yard) rail with gravel ballast. Between Omaha and Kansas City the country is fairly flat with a considerable amount of soft marshy territory through which the railroad runs. It is on this territory that the steam engine is showing destructive effect on the track. The Burlington made calculations as to how fast it would be advisable to operate the Zephyr over these lines and then made test runs to check their calculations. A few modifications were made and special speed boards were installed for the Zephyr's operation. These speed boards have an illuminated "Z" of the reflector button type such as we use for state highway route numbers in Massachusetts. Under this illuminated "Z" is the speed restriction of 45, 60, or 85 miles per hour as the case may be. These restrictions go into effect 3,000 feet beyond the installation of the board. The Operating men and Engineers consider them invaluable because the undertaking of running a new piece of equipment such as the Zephyr involves so much that it would be very burdensome to have to remember speed restriction by bulletin order.

Because the Burlington has in mind the operation of several more of these high speed streamline trains they have one man assigned to the Zephyr at all times solely for the purpose of collecting data regarding traffic, public opinion, performance data, etc. I believe that this is a necessary part of the operation of high speed streamline trains in order that we may know as far as possible whether we are shooting in the right direction or not.

Each passenger is given a souvenir ticket as he leaves the train and this little detail seems to be appreciated as our 74* passengers who received these tickets at Kansas City, there was not one who threw this ticket away.

This train is maintained at Lincoln, Neb., during the night. During the exhibition tour, the entire train was washed with Bonami each day but this has been discontinued and the car is simply dry wiped each night. They feel about once each two months (it) will be necessary to give it a good washing and polishing, but that the dry wiping will take care of it during this interim. The inside of the car is vacuum cleaned and swept, floors washed, etc. each night and at the end of 45,000 miles of operation is in extremely good and clean condition.

One of the biggest troubles on this train is the mat-

route and remained in that service through October 23, 1938.

On June 8, 1934, less than two months after the introduction of the Burlington Zephyr, the Boston & Maine Railroad placed a $280,000 order with the Edward G. Budd Company of Philadelphia for one 600 hp, three-car articulated stainless steel streamliner with GM/Winton diesel power and GE electrical gear.

A $225,000 Federal Reconstruction Finance Corporation loan covering 80% of its purchase price was approved in August, and construction began. The first streamliner east of the Mississippi was completed in late January 1935 and arrived at the B&M's Mechanicville, New York yard on February 9, 1935. Nearly identical to the Zephyr, the 113-ton, 199'-long stainless steel streamliner was promptly exhibited across the "jointly managed" B&M and Maine Central systems with numerous "trips to nowhere and back" for the local citizenry over the next two months.

Boston & Maine's $280,000 three-car, 132-seat Flying Yankee was a sister to the Pioneer Zephyr, entering service in the East in April of 1935. Here it is posed at the Budd Company in February of 1935.

B&M #6000, christened the Flying Yankee, entered service between Boston, Portland and Bangor on April 4, 1935. The 132-seat speedster cut an hour and a half off the Boston to Bangor run, covered 733 miles per day six days a week, and brought passengers back to the B&M and MEC in droves. The Flying Yankee, immediately and irreverently nicknamed the "Tin Fish," was, like its older Zephyr sibling, a sellout success.

On June 28, 1938 the fourth car, #525, was removed from the Zephyr and a new buffet-dinette-chair car, #500, was sub-

stituted. Car #505, originally delivered as a baggage-buffet-chair car was gutted and converted to a full baggage car, although the original window configuration was retained.

CB&Q #9900 was assigned to Trains #32 and #33, the Ozark State Zephyr between October 24, 1938 and April 29, 1939. After a brief shopping and "spring cleaning," it returned to its original Lincoln-Kansas City assignment on May 2, 1939.

Tragedy struck #9900 on October 2, 1939 when the Pioneer Zephyr ran an open switch at Napier, Missouri and collided head on at 50 mph with 2-8-2 type steam locomotive #4973 and its freight in the siding. Both crewmen in the Zephyr's cab were killed, and the carbody was returned on a flatcar to the Aurora shops for repairs.

Repaired better than new by the Aurora shops thanks to substantial assistance from both Budd and Electro-Motive, #9900 reached its million mile of service at 9:18 a.m. near Council Bluffs, Iowa on December 29, 1939.

In March and April of 1940 the little train first substituted for the Sam Houston Zephyr between Forth Worth and Houston, followed by a couple of weeks on its original assignment, and then served as the Mark Twain Zephyr between St. Louis and Kansas City as well.

SELLS WAR BONDS

On April 30, 1940 #9900 entered service as Trains #43 and #44 between St. Louis and Burlington, Iowa. It remained

The Union Pacific Railroad's new three-car M-10000 Pullman-Standard-built train was North America's first streamliner, delivered to the UP in February of 1934. Here the Pioneer Zephyr and the M-10000 meet at Kansas City Union Station in 1935.

in this assignment through February 1943 when it toured Nebraska to help sell U.S. War Bonds. Its war bond assignment completed, beginning on March 8, 1943 the Zephyr began service as Trains #5 and #22 between Lincoln and McCook, Nebraska that lasted through June of 1948.

A grand party was thrown in Lincoln, Nebraska on April 10, 1944 for the granddaddy of the CB&Q's now-extensive Zephyr fleet. Standing beside freshly delivered 456-ton, 5,400 hp Electro-Motive Division Model FT freight locomotive CB&Q #102, the little streamliner slowly advanced toward its giant 1,000-pound birthday cake, and in so doing sliced the cake with an 8' long stainless steel (what else?) knife specially designed for the occasion. Guests of honor included Ralph Budd, Edward Budd and Charles Kettering. The diminutive Pioneer Zephyr showed little evidence of having traveled 1,679,000 miles in service over the prior decade. The two-cycle chant of the engines in both the Zephyr and the giant freight locomotive beside it confirmed their family relationship.

Only seven months after its birthday bash the Pioneer Zephyr was rammed from the rear at Fairmont, Nebraska on November 12, 1944 by nearly new Burlington Route FT set #105 leading Denver-bound time freight #61. The observation section, about 20 feet, was virtually destroyed and the Zephyr went to the Aurora shops for repairs. Consideration

was given to substituting the parlor-observation from #9901, the power unit of which burned a few days later on December 16, 1944 in Texas, but ultimately the parlor-observation was rebuilt and #9900 returned to service between Lincoln and McCook, Nebraska through June of 1948.

RAILROAD FAIR

The Pioneer Zephyr returned to lakefront Chicago between July 1 and October 4, 1948 as the premier exhibit of the "Q's" display at the Chicago Railroad Fair. Its winter assignment began November 14 as Trains #11 and #12 between Houston and Fort Worth, Texas. Unfortunately #9900 hit a cement mixer at Houston on April 29, 1949 and had to return to the Aurora shops for repair. Repairs completed, the #9900 went back to the Chicago Railroad Fair between August 27 and September 30, 1949.

The date of April 29 was not a good one for the Pioneer Zephyr. After the 1949 Chicago Railroad Fair closed, #9900 was assigned as Trains #31 and #32 between Denver and Cheyenne beginning October 15, 1949. On April 29, 1950 it hit a truck at Longmont, Colorado, killing the fireman, and once again returned to Aurora shops for repairs. At this time the four-car, buffet-dinette-chair car #500 was removed and stored.

From October 18, 1950 through January 31, 1953 the Pio-

Following the popularity of the Pioneer Zephyr, in quick order the Burlington began christening more Zephyrs, including the Twin Zephyrs, the Denver Zephyrs and Mark Twain Zephyr, among others. The Pioneer Zephyr, with its new oscillating Mars warning light above its headlight, stops at Longmont, Colorado on October 16, 1949. *J. Michael Gruber collection*

Serial Number Salvation, or from Scrap to the Smithsonian

The first four articulated Zephyrs shared virtually identical power plants, as did the EMC/Winton 600 hp S, SC, or SW model yard switchers owned by the Burlington Route. A power plant in need of major repair could, and was, quickly switched out and replaced by a previously rebuilt one, thus minimizing the time any of the articulated streamline trains were out of service.

Accordingly, the Pioneer Zephyr had at least two, if not more, individual Winton Model 201A 8-cylinder engines installed in it during its operational lifetime. Winton serial #4510 was the prime mover in the Zephyr when it was delivered, and performed its record-breaking run. For some reason, most likely premature excessive wear, this engine was removed in May 1936, returned to EMC/Winton and replaced with a new one, serial #4686. The original engine was rebuilt by EMC/Winton and installed in a new 600 hp switcher delivered to Great Lakes Steel in 1937.

REMOVE WINTON ENGINE

Electro-Motive received Great Lake Steel's model SW switcher #6 at LaGrange, Illinois in August 1956 for rebuilding to current standards. While stripping the old engine and associated equipment from the locomotive frame, somebody checked the Winton engine serial number against original records and realized that the original record-breaking prime mover of the as-delivered Burlington Zephyr was now in the process of being removed by EMD shop men as scrap.

After several impromptu discussions and phone calls, the worn, oil- and grime-encrusted Winton 201A engine that a few hours earlier was destined for Pielet Bros reclamation yard adjacent to EMD was set aside for preservation.

Nearly eight years later, on June 30, 1964 Electro-Motive Division General Manager / General Motors Vice President Richard L. Terrell and Smithsonian Director Frank A. Taylor officiated at a ceremony in the Smithsonian Institution in Washington, D.C. Belatedly, the Winton Model 201A engine that powered the Zephyr on its May 26, 1934 record Denver-Chicago run was placed on display in the transportation section of America's Attic. It remains there today as an American engineering and industrial icon.

Its preservation was apparently due solely to fate and a historically minded Electro-Motive employee and his management.

This is an overview of Train #31 as it pulls into at Longmont, Colorado, on October 16, 1949 over subsidiary Colorado & Southern Railway. The Pioneer Zephyr maintained the Denver to Cheyenne, Wyoming run from October 15, 1949 to April 29, 1950. *J. Michael Gruber collection*

neer Zephyr served as Trains #6 and #11 between Galesburg and Quincy, Illinois. It connected with two of its younger siblings, the westbound California Zephyr and the eastbound Nebraska Zephyr.

The #9900 was reassigned on February 1, 1953 to Trains #3 and #4 in service between Galesburg, Quincy and St. Joseph. Sibling #9903 was assigned to the opposite side of the daily service that lasted through August of 1957.

The Pioneer Zephyr's final assignment was as Trains #41 and #44 between St. Joseph and Lincoln from August 1957 through February 20, 1960. On March 20, 1960 the Pioneer Zephyr carried a full load of loyal railroad enthusiasts from Lincoln to Galesburg to celebrate its retirement from regular service. In 25 years and 10 months the Zephyr had traveled 3,222,898 miles.

NEAR-NEW CONDITION

For one final time the Pioneer Zephyr visited Aurora shops where it was cleaned, painted, and restored to near-new condition. Baggage-buffet-chair car #505 was returned to its as-delivered interior configuration with the installation of interior partitions, buffet equipment, and 20 leather-covered smoking section seats.

On May 3, 1960 the Zephyr traveled its last rail miles from Aurora to the Illinois Central team tracks at Hyde Park Bou-

1st regular service trip of the **ZEPHYR**

Lincoln, Omaha, Council Bluffs, St. Joseph and Kansas City

Nov. 11, 1934

Burlington Route

1st Diesel-powered streamline train in America to be established in daily operation

This cachet applied in the Railway Postal Car while the Zephyr was en route on the first trip

levard, Chicago. Several days later its three car body sections were separated and individually trucked to Chicago's Museum of Science and Industry on lowbed trailers.

On May 26, 1960 the original three-car Pioneer Zephyr was formally donated to Chicago's Museum of Science and Industry when Burlington Route President Harry Murphy handed over #9900's throttle with due fanfare to Museum President Major Lenox R. Lohr.

In silent witness to how brief the streamline era had been, along with Museum and GM's Electro-Motive Division officials, both Jack Ford—who piloted the Zephyr when new to numerous speed records, and Ms. Marguerite Cotsworth—who had christened the train 26 years earlier, were in attendance at the dedication ceremony. Even President Murphy was there, who had been on the Zephyr's record Denver-Chicago run 26 years earlier to the day.

The decline of the streamline era accelerated throughout the 1960's. On March 2, 1970 the Burlington Route was no more, having merged with the Great Northern, Northern Pacific and Spokane, Seattle & Pacific railroads into the new Burlington Northern Railroad. The Zephyr fleet itself faded into history less than a year later, on May 1, 1971, when BN turned its streamliners over to a quasi-governmental entity, Amtrak.

During the second annual convention of the National Model Railroad Association in Chicago in July of 1936, a group of members toured the Zephyr pit and #9900 at Burlington facilities near the Loop. *J. Michael Gruber collection*

With the second anniversary of the Pioneer Zephyr, the proud Burlington and the public together celebrated 24 months of bliss. The Zephyr had carried 120,000 passengers, racking up more than 420,000 service miles. Nameplates with *Pioneer Zephyr* emblazoned on them were attached to the train's observation lounge car.

On June 28, 1938 the fourth car of the Zephyr, #525, was removed and a new buffet-dinette-chair car, #500, was substituted. Here the four-car Zephyr zips along Burlington rails in its early days.

Townspeople of Longmont, Colorado line up to tour the Pioneer Zephyr. Note the white flags on the cab, indicating a special train. *J. Michael Gruber collection*

The Advance Zephyrs—1,039 miles overnight between Chicago and Denver—were no-extra-fare trains. They could accommodate only 60 coach passengers and thus were nearly always booked. Later, Denver Zephyr equipment arrived, including an A-B power set and ten passenger cars including four sleepers. This new train featured named cars, all beginning with the word "Silver." *Don Heimburger collection*

Always seeking promotional opportunities for the railroad and its new train, the Burlington exhibited a mock-up of the Pioneer Zephyr at the Texas Centennial in 1936. Note the Art Deco style of the train and the lettering above.

LEFT. On the occasion of the Zephyr's 10th birthday, the railroad held a party in Lincoln, Nebraska on April 10, 1944. The Zephyr began moving forward, which in turn cut a cord that caused a giant stainless-steel knife to slice through a 1,000-pound birthday cake. On the far side of the tent are Edward Budd and Ralph Budd. ABOVE. A close-up of the Pioneer Zephyr's 660-hp Winton engine.

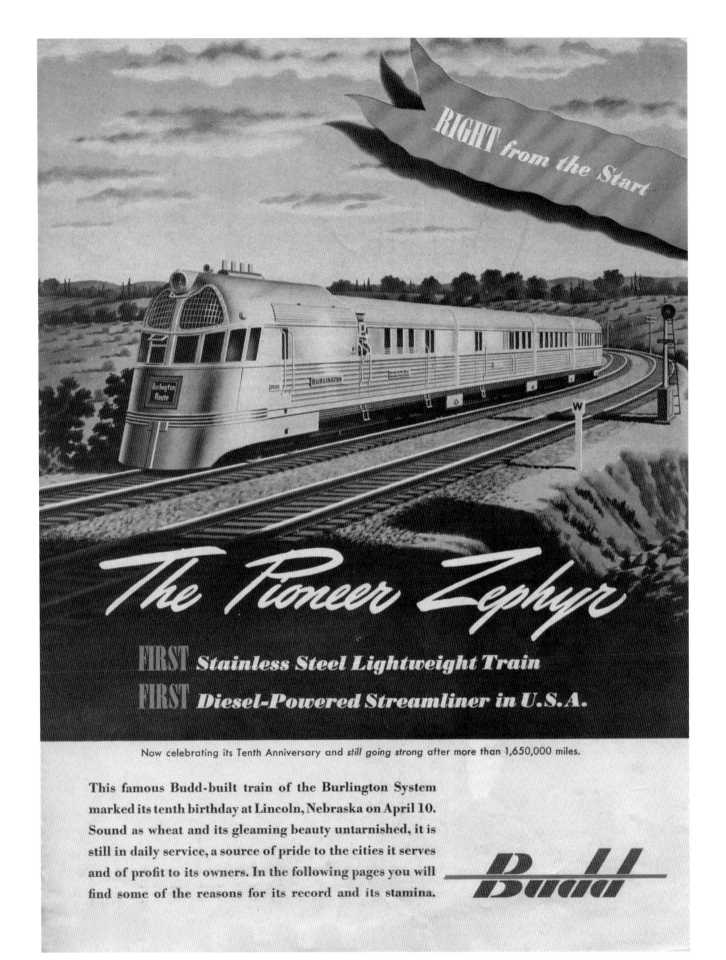

RIGHT *from the Start*

The Pioneer Zephyr

FIRST **Stainless Steel Lightweight Train**
FIRST **Diesel-Powered Streamliner in U.S.A.**

Now celebrating its Tenth Anniversary and *still going strong* after more than 1,650,000 miles.

This famous Budd-built train of the Burlington System marked its tenth birthday at Lincoln, Nebraska on April 10. Sound as wheat and its gleaming beauty untarnished, it is still in daily service, a source of pride to the cities it serves and of profit to its owners. In the following pages you will find some of the reasons for its record and its stamina.

Budd

The Budd Company of Philadelphia was rightly proud of its participation in and construction of the Pioneer Zephyr, and on the occasion of the 10th birthday of the Zephyr, produced this advertisement.

The four-car Pioneer Zephyr, expanded from the three-car 1934 Zephyr in 1936, and later spawned many more stainless-steel streamlined Zephyrs. By 1944, all the Zephyrs combined had traveled more than 22 million miles. *Bombardier, Don Heimburger collection*

This four-page brochure, issued by the Burlington on the tenth anniversary of the Pioneer Zephyr, states: "Today I celebrated my tenth birthday... they threw a swell birthday party for me in the morning at the Burlington Station and a lot of big shots and half of Lincoln (Nebraska) were there. Maybe you heard it broadcast over the Blue Network. Believe it or not, I cut my own birthday cake, and was it a whopper!"

THE *Zephyr* FLEET

Since the Pioneer Zephyr took to the rails ten years ago, as America's first diesel-powered, streamline train, the Burlington has added many more Zephyrs to its fleet. Today, there are fourteen of them, serving wartime America, efficiently and speedily. Their mileage record is shown below.

	TOTAL MILEAGE TO APRIL 10, 1944
Pioneer Zephyr	1,679,169
Sam Houston Zephyr	1,928,182
Texas Rocket	1,941,841
Mark Twain Zephyr	1,557,303
Twin Zephyrs (2 trains)	4,597,617
Denver Zephyrs (2 trains)	5,566,261
Silver Streak Zephyr	951,928
General Pershing Zephyr	640,851
Ak-Sar-Ben Zephyr	669,926
Zephyr Rocket	672,400
Texas Zephyrs (2 trains)	2,201,203
Total, All Zephyrs	22,406,681

Burlington Route

THE PIONEER *Zephyr*

April 10, 1944

Dear Buddy:

Today I celebrated my tenth birthday—and what a party! The blow-out was in Lincoln, Nebraska, my present eastern terminus, where I started in 1934 as the first streamline train in regular service in America.

They threw a swell birthday party for me in the morning at the Burlington Station and a lot of big shots and half of Lincoln were there. Maybe you heard it broadcast over the Blue Network. Believe it or not, I cut my own birthday cake, and was it a whopper! Most of it went to kids and service men in Lincoln hospitals, but I saved out enough to send a piece to you and all my other younger brothers.

Then at noontime, the Lincoln Chamber of Commerce gave a luncheon at which a lot of nice things were said about us diesel-powered and streamline trains. Governor Griswold and Mayor Marti were on the reception end. Good talks by Edward G. Budd, my builder; Charles F. Kettering, of General Motors, who diesel-ed me; Ralph Budd, my boss, and Gen. Charles G. Dawes, former Vice President of the United States.

I wish you could have been there but I know that you, like myself, are too busy these days to leave your wartime job to go galavanting off to birthday parties.

Your Pal,

Pioneer Zephyr

P.S. More dope on my birthday party on the inside pages ———→

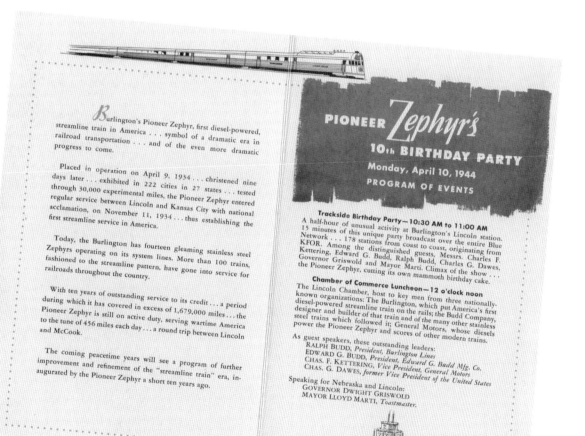

Burlington's Pioneer Zephyr, first diesel-powered, streamline train in America . . . symbol of a dramatic era in railroad transportation . . . and of the even more dramatic progress to come.

Placed in operation on April 9, 1934 . . . christened nine days later . . . exhibited in 222 cities in 27 states . . . tested through 30,000 experimental miles, the Pioneer Zephyr entered regular service between Lincoln and Kansas City with national acclamation, on November 11, 1934 . . . thus establishing the first streamline service in America.

Today, the Burlington has fourteen gleaming stainless steel Zephyrs operating on its system lines. More than 100 trains, fashioned to the streamline pattern, have gone into service for railroads throughout the country.

With ten years of outstanding service to its credit . . . a period during which it has covered in excess of 1,679,000 miles . . . the Pioneer Zephyr is still on active duty, serving wartime America to the tune of 456 miles each day . . . a round trip between Lincoln and McCook.

The coming peacetime years will see a program of further improvement and refinement of the "streamline train" era, inaugurated by the Pioneer Zephyr a short ten years ago.

PIONEER *Zephyr's* 10th BIRTHDAY PARTY
Monday, April 10, 1944
PROGRAM OF EVENTS

Trackside Birthday Party—10:30 AM to 11:00 AM
A half-hour of unusual activity at Burlington's Lincoln station. 15 minutes of this unique party broadcast over the entire Blue Network . . . 178 stations from coast to coast, originating from KFOR. Among the distinguished guests, Messrs. Charles F. Kettering, Edward G. Budd, Ralph Budd, Charles G. Dawes, Governor Griswold and Mayor Marti. Climax of the show . . . the Pioneer Zephyr, cutting its own mammoth birthday cake.

Chamber of Commerce Luncheon—12 o'clock noon
The Lincoln Chamber, host to key men from three nationally-known organizations: The Burlington, which put America's first diesel-powered streamline train on the rails; the Budd Company, designer and builder of that train and of the many other stainless steel trains which followed it; General Motors, whose diesels power the Pioneer Zephyr and scores of other modern trains.

As guest speakers, these outstanding leaders:
RALPH BUDD, President, Burlington Lines
EDWARD G. BUDD, President, Edward G. Budd Mfg. Co.
CHAS. F. KETTERING, Vice President, General Motors
CHAS. G. DAWES, former Vice President of the United States

Speaking for Nebraska and Lincoln:
GOVERNOR DWIGHT GRISWOLD
MAYOR LLOYD MARTI, Toastmaster.

This photo of the Zephyr was taken in Toledo, Ohio, on May 3, 1934 by the Budd Company photographer. The steam locomotive water column is on borrowed time. *Bombardier, Don Heimburger collection*

The sister to the Pioneer Zephyr was the Flying Yankee, shown here northbound to Bangor, Maine on the Maine Central Railroad at Portland, Maine. The train was delivered to the Maine Central in February of 1935. *Don Heimburger collection*

ABOVE. The Pioneer Zephyr's unique truck skirts are seen clearly in this picture taken at Quincy, Illinois in 1952. The train ran between Quincy and Chicago. *Philip Weibler* BELOW. The Zephyr stops to discharge and load passengers during one of its early runs. Note the large Mars light. *Don Heimburger collection*

Zipping past Iowa cornfields south of Council Bluffs, Iowa in the summer of 1935, the four-car Pioneer Zephyr was the result of increased ridership of from 50 to 100% over steam-operated trains. *Don Heimburger collection*

ABOVE. The Zephyr fleet cumulatively reached one million miles on May 27, 1936, near Savanna, Illinois. That same day, Zephyr #9902 did the honors as Ralph Budd spoke to the Chicago Association of Commerce about this milestone. *Chris Burritt collection*

BELOW. The Pioneer Zephyr, with an added Mars light, awaits orders to leave West Quincy, Missouri's Burlington station in 1953. The Burlington started using the West Quincy station in January of 1953. *Philip Weibler*

The Pioneer Zephyr in Detail

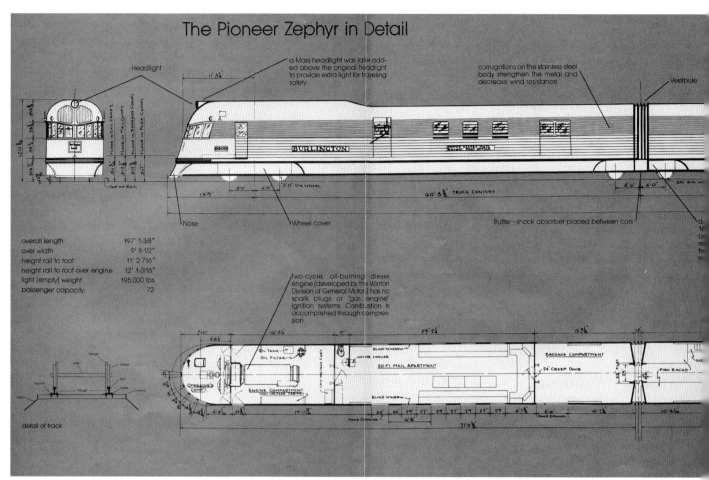

overall length — 197' 1-3/8"
over width — 9' 8-1/2"
height rail to roof — 11' 2-7/16"
height rail to roof over engine — 12' 1-3/16"
light (empty) weight — 195,000 lbs.
passenger capacity — 72

BELOW. The Pioneer Zephyr, on the right, and the Mark Twain Zephyr, arrive at the Quincy, Illinois passenger station at the same time in the fall of 1952. NEXT PAGE, RIGHT. In another photograph looking from the opposite direction, the Pioneer Zephyr and the Mark Twain Zephyr show their respective tailsigns. The end cars featured a combined backup and Mars light in the middle and marker lamps on each side. Both photos, *Philip Weibler*

94

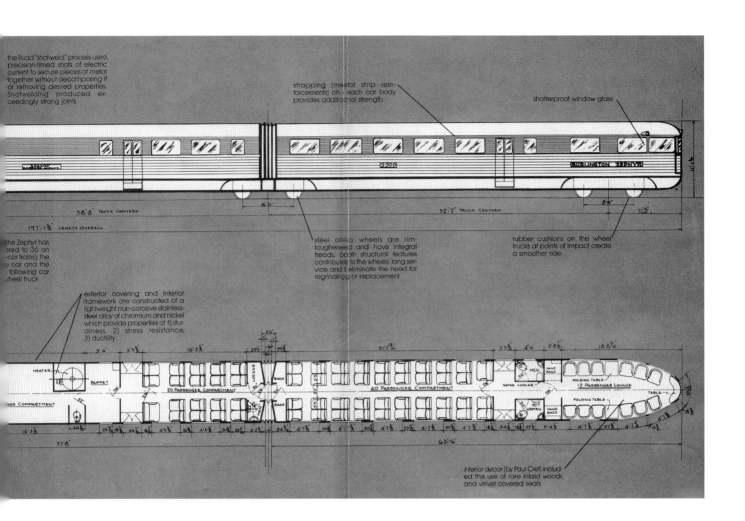

the Budd "shot-weld" process used precision-timed shots of electric current to secure pieces of metal together without decomposing it or removing desired properties. Shotwelding produced exceedingly strong joints

strapping (metal strip reinforcements) on each car body provides additional strength

shatterproof window glass

58'-8" TRUCK CENTERS

52'-7" TRUCK CENTERS

8'-0"

11'-5"

197'-1⅜" LENGTH OVERALL

the Zephyr has ...ared to 36 on ...-car trains); the ... car and the ... following car ...wheel truck

steel all-loy wheels are rim-toughened and have integral treads; both structural features contributes to the wheels' long service and eliminate the need for regrinding or replacement

rubber cushions on the wheel trucks at points of impact create a smoother ride

exterior covering and interior framework are constructed of a lightweight non-corrosive stainless-steel alloy of chromium and nickel which provide properties of 1) sturdiness, 2) stress resistance, 3) ductility

HEATER

BUFFET

70 PASSENGER COMPARTMENT

LOCKER

BAGS

BAGS

40 PASSENGER COMPARTMENT

WATER COOLER

MEN

WOMEN

HAND BAGS

HAND BAGS

FOLDING TABLE

FOLDING TABLE

12 PASSENGER LOUNGE

TABLE

...AGE COMPARTMENT

57'-8"

65'-6"

interior decor (by Paul Cret) included the use of rare inlaid woods and velvet covered seats

Showing the train's tailsign and the huge backup and Mars warning lights now in place on the Pioneer Zephyr, this end view also reveals how the large windows in the solarium lounge provided excellent views. *Philip Weibler*

First Month of Zephyr Brings Traffic Increase

Burlington officers report also that it has taken little from other trains

The operation of the Zephyr of the Chicago, Burlington & Quincy between Lincoln, Nebraska and Kansas City, Missouri, during its first 30-day period, resulted in increased passenger business. During this period, the schedule was maintained each day, except westbound into Lincoln on four days when there were slight delays due to interference of the other trains and on one occasion when the Zephyr was hit by a farmer's truck. Between Omaha, Neb. and Lincoln in both directions, the number of passengers carried increased 111 per cent, as compared with the traffic on steam trains in October, 1934. Southbound passengers leaving Omaha and Council Bluffs for all points averaged 49 per trip, as compared with 26 on steam trains in October, an increase of 88 per cent. Southbound into Kansas City, passengers from all points averaged 60 per trip, as compared with 35 during October, an increase of 71 per cent. Northbound out of Kansas City, passengers for all points averaged 57 per trip, as compared with 31 during October, an increase of 84 per cent. Northbound into Council Bluffs and Omaha, passengers from all points averaged 49 per trip, as compared with 21 during October, an increase of 135 per cent.

The total number of passengers between any points in both directions averaged 105 per trip, as compared with 62 during October, an increase of 69 per cent, but the average distance traveled per passenger was greater on the Zephyr than on the steam trains, because passengers carried one mile per train-mile on the Zephyr during this 30-day period averaged 29 as compared with 25 on the steam trains during October, an increase of 96 per cent.

According to officers of the road the Zephyr has taken little traffic away from the other trains—two in each direction. The passengers carried one mile per train-mile on the four steam trains decreased 24 per cent in November, 1933 as compared with October, 1933 whereas the passengers carried one mile per train-mile decreased only 7.6 per cent in November, 1934, as compared with October 1934.

The 72 seats on the Zephyr were inadequate on six southbound and four northbound trips. On November 28, ninety nine passengers were on the train at one time, while 6 of the 10 trips exceeded 80. On December 2, a steam train supplemented the Zephyr service, due to holiday traffic, carrying northbound 183 passengers in addition to the total of 144 carried on the Zephyr. Since December 7, this supplementary steam service has been operating daily in both directions, primarily to handle increased volume of U.S. mail and the express.

As passengers on the Zephyr present their tickets, the conductor asks, "Are you riding this train because it is the Zephyr or would you be making a trip at this particular time if this were an ordinary steam train instead of the Zephyr?" During the 25-day period, 58 per cent of the persons replying said they would have used an ordinary train at that time, 17 per cent would have used some other steam trains except for the Zephyr, 13 would have used an automobile, bus or airplane and 12 per cent would not have been making the trip at all and were merely riding the Zephyr out of curiosity. During the first five days of operation the latter group amounted to 67 per cent. *December 22, 1934 Railway Age*

Partial List of Equipment and Specialties on the 1934 Pioneer Zephyr

Builder .... Edward G. Budd Mfg. Co., Philadelphia, PA
Stainless Steel .... Alleghany Steel Co., Brackenridge, PA
American Sheet & Tin Plate Co., Pittsburgh, PA
American Steel & Wire Co., Chicago, IL
Republic Steel Corp., Youngstown, Ohio
Superior Steel Co., Pittsburgh, PA
Helical volute springs .... Cyrus J. Holland, Chicago, IL
Elliptic springs .... Mather Spring Co., Toledo, Ohio
Coil springs .... American Steel Foundries, Chicago, IL
Brake rigging and brake shoes
American Brake Shoe & Foundry Co., New York
Engine bed .... Lukenweld, Inc., Coatesville, PA
Truck and body articulation castings
General Steel Castings Corp., Eddystone, PA
Wheels and axles .... Bethlehem Steel Co., Bethlehem, PA
Side bearings .... A. Stucki Co., Pittsburgh, PA
Axle bearings .... Timken Roller Bearing Co., Canton, Ohio
Rubber insulation .... U. S. Rubber Co., New York
Rubber bumpers .... Quaker City Rubber Co., Philadelphia, PA
Rubber .... Continental Rubber Co., Erie, PA
Dryden Rubber Co., Chicago, IL
Goodrich Rubber Co., Akron, Ohio
Air brakes .... Westinghouse Air Brake Co., Wilmerding, PA
Hand brakes .... National Brake Co., Buffalo, NY
Flexible metal hose .... American Flexible Metallic
Tubing Co., Philadelphia, PA
Flexible metal hose .... Pennsylvania Flexible Metallic
Tubing Co., Philadelphia, PA
Couplers .... McConway & Torley Corp., Pittsburgh, PA
Equalizer .... Camden Forge Co., Camden, NJ
Power plant, complete .... Winton Engine Co., Cleveland, Ohio
Oil pump .... Viking Pump Co., Cedar Falls, Iowa
Oil radiators .... Young Radiator Co., Racine, WI
Ventilating fans .... B. F. Sturtevant Co., Boston, MA
V-belt .... Dayton Rubber Co., Dayton, Ohio
Sidelining .... Masonite Corp., Chicago, IL
Headlining .... Agasote Milboard Co., Trenton, NJ
Weatherstripping .... Midgley & Borrowdale, Chicago, IL
Insulation .... Alfol Insulation Co., New York
Felt .... Fidelity Felt Co., Philadelphia, PA
Diaphragms between cars .... Morton Mfg. Co., Chicago, IL
Lounge chairs and tables
S. Karpen Bros., Chicago, IL furnished by Mandel Bros., Chicago, IL
Seats and partitions .... Hale & Kilburn, Philadelphia, PA
Seat covering and carpets
L. C. Chase Co., New York, furnished by Mandel Bros., Chicago, IL
Copper screen .... Newark Wire Cloth Co., Newark, NJ
Rubber weatherstrip .... Manhattan Rubber Co., Passaic, NJ
Sash .... O.M. Edwards Co., Syracuse, NY
Window glass .... Pittsburgh Plate Glass Co., Pittsburgh, PA
Door locks .... Russell Erwin Co., New Britain, Conn.
Door tracks and hangers .... Richards-Wilcox Co., Aurora, IL
Hinges .... Homer D. Bronson, Beacon Falls, Conn.
Soss Mfg. Co., Roselle, NJ
Stanley Works, New Britain, Conn.
Castings (assist door handles) .... American Chain Co., Bridgeport, Conn.
Plymetl dead light panels .... US Plywood Co., New York
Insulation and fibrous adhesive .... Johns-Manville Co., New York
Lumber .... Sykes Lumber Co., Philadelphia, PA
Molding .... Herron-Zimmer Molding Co., Detroit, MI
Martin Parry Co., York, PA
Cork floor .... Armstrong Cork and Insulation Co., Lancaster, PA
Stainless steel engine-cooling grille ... Tuttle & Baily, New Britain, Conn.

Buffet .... Angelo Colonna, Philadelphia, PA
Table tops .... Formica Insulation Co., Cincinnati, Ohio
Air conditioning and cooling .... York Ice Machinery Corp, York, PA
All pipe insulation .... Keasbey & Mattison Co., Ambler, PA
Air duct insulation .... Celotex Co., Chicago, IL
Air filter .... Brillo Mfg. Co., Philadelphia, PA
Freon refrigerant .... Kinetic Chemicals Co., Wilmington, Del.
Exhaust fans .... Robbins & Meyers Co., Springfield, Ohio
Air conditioning grilles .... Uni-Flo Grille Corp., Detroit, MI
Heating and cooling controls .... Pennsylvania Electric Switch Co.,
Des Moines, IA
Heating plant and thermo-static controls
Vapor Car Heating Co., Chicago, IL
Radiation .... J. A. Nesbitt, Inc., Philadelphia, PA
Conduit fittings .... Crouse-Hinds Co., Syracuse, NY
Storage batteries .... Electric Storage Battery Co., Philadelphia, PA
Electrical fittings .... Arrow, Hart & Hegeman Co., Hartford, Conn.
Electric power equipment .... General Electric Co., Schenectady, NY
Air compressors
Auxiliary battery charging generator
Electric grills and urns
Bearings on main driving motors, ventilating equipment and air-brake
equipment .... S.K.F. Industries, Inc., Philadelphia, PA
Lamp bulbs .... National Lamp Co., Cleveland, Ohio
Lamp regulator and fixtures
Safety Car Heating & Lighting Co., New York
Fans in railway post office
Conduit and light fittings .... Taplet Mfg. Co., Philadelphia, PA
Fuse blocks .... Trumbull Electric Co., Plainville, Conn.
Nofuze load center .. Westinghouse Elec. & Mfg. Co., East Pittsburgh, PA
Wire .... Gilby Wire Co., Newark, NJ
Okonite Co., New York
Drape curtain rods .... Kirsch Co., Sturgis, MI
Curtain material (drapes) .... Bassett McNabe Co., Philadelphia, PA
Rolled curtains .... Adams & Westlake Co., Chicago, IL
Curtains .... Pantasote Co., New York
Waterproof carpet runner .... John Wanamaker, Philadelphia, PA
Lamps and smoking stand .... Gaumer Biddle, Philadelphia, PA
Radio .... Stromberg-Carlson Tele. Mfg. Co., Rochester, NY
Converter for radio .... Electric Specialty Co., Stamford, Conn.
Special fittings .... Crane Co., Chicago, IL
Piping and fittings .... Chase Brass & Copper Co., Waterbury, Conn.
Lavatory equipment .... Dayton Mfg. Co., Dayton, Ohio
Paper cups and dispensers .... Logan Drinking Cup Company,
Worchester, Mass., Division of United States Envelope Company
Paper towels and cabinets .... Northern Paper Mills, Green Bay, NY
Water coolers .... Henry Giessel Co., Chicago, IL
Enamel, baggage room, post office, engine room .... Larkin Co., Inc.,
Buffalo, NY
Speedometer .... Weston Electrical Instrument Co., Newark, NJ
Sanders .... Graham-White Sander Co., Roanoke, VA
Signal valve .... National Pneumatic Co., New York
Whistle valves .... Lunkenheimer Co., Cincinnati, Ohio
Tyfon horns .... Leslie Mfg. Co., Lyndhurst, NJ
Monel screws and nuts .... International Nickel Co., New York
Fibre nuts .... Elastic Stop Nut Corp., Elizabeth, NJ
Head and back-up lights .... Electric Service Supplies, Philadelphia, PA
Marker and classification lights, conduits and light fittings ....
.... Pyle-National Co., Chicago, IL
Oilite center bearing plates .... Amplex Mfg. Co., Detroit, MI
Clear vision mechanism .... Motor Products Corp., Detroit, MI

April 14, 1934 Railway Age

April 21, 1935

In the very competitive Chicago to Twin Cities passenger market, the Burlington unleashed the Twin Zephyrs, which went head to head with trains of the Milwaukee Road and the Chicago & NorthWestern. Here the Twins are on a pre-inaugural run between Aurora and Chicago on April 14, 1935. Each side-by-side train contains 44 human twins!

Chapter 7

— Siblings Galore! —
The Zephyr Fleet Arrives

Before the Pioneer Zephyr turned a wheel in revenue service the Burlington Route in July 1934 inked a $500,000 purchase order to the Budd Company for two more "three car stainless steel Zephyr-type streamline trains" for Chicago-Twin Cities service.

These twin trains had no RPO compartment, but more seats—88—than the initial design. They also were the first Zephyrs to use Westinghouse's newly-developed HSC high-speed electrically actuated pneumatic air brakes. Twin Zephyr #9901 was accepted by the CB&Q in Philadelphia on March 23, 1935, followed on April 10 by Twin Zephyr #9902.

TWIN ZEPHYRS

Once again the Burlington's Publicity Department went into high gear, and the two silvery speedsters were photographed and exhibited galore. Their most memorable stunt was the side-by-side operation of #9901 and #9902 on April 14, 1935 from Aurora, Illinois down the triple-track speedway to Chicago Union Station carrying 44 sets of human twins. The following day, April 15, 1935 the Twin Zephyrs were christened at Chicago Union Station by twins Marion and Frances Beeler, and the trains entered revenue service on April 21.

Demand for space on the new Twin Zephyrs was so great that on June 2, 1935 both sets were placed in daily roundtrip service. Each covered 882 miles per day, and the pair averaged 97% availability the first year. With the reduction in running time from 10 hours to first 6 1/2 hours and later to 6 hours flat, demand became so great that steam-powered second sections were run on a regular basis, and people were regularly turned away from the sold out trains. The great Chicago to Twin Cities competition between the Burlington, the Chicago & NorthWestern, and the Milwaukee Road was at hand.

The fourth, and final articulated Zephyr entered service on October 28, 1935 between St. Louis and Burlington, Iowa. Christened the Mark Twain Zephyr on October 25, 1935 by Samuel Clement's granddaughter, Miss Nina Gabrilowitsch, the Zephyr was named in honor of its route beside the Mississippi and through the American author's hometown of Hannibal, Missouri.

The power car was named Injun Joe, for that character in Mark Twain's immortal classics *Huckleberry Finn* and *Tom Sawyer*. The power car name was also chosen as a play on words between Engine and Injun. The second car was baggage only and named Becky Thatcher; the third was a buffet-chair car and named Huckleberry Finn; while the fourth was named Tom Sawyer and contained both coach and parlor observation seating. The Mark Twain Zephyr was the first Zephyr delivered new as a four-car set.

Thanks to overwhelming public response and profitability of their new Zephyrs, the Burlington Passenger Department's thoughts turned to longer, more important runs. Top on the list was the 400-mile Twin Cities-Chicago market where existing passenger demand had completely overwhelmed the little three-car Zephyrs. Accordingly, the "Q" in the late fall of 1935 issued AFE #28256 to Budd for two fully articulated six-car trains ($887,582.66) and two individual 1,800 hp shovelnose locomotives from EMC ($366,648.88) to power them.

Next under consideration was the 1,000-mile overnight run between Denver and Chicago. There the Burlington competed head to head with the Union Pacific, and the UP had just announced its order for two 10-car passenger train sets complete with twin diesel-electric powered locomotives. They were to be constructed of riveted aluminum and steel respectively by Pullman-Standard. Each locomotive would contain a 1,200 hp V-16 Winton engine and controls supplied by EMC for a total of 2,400 horsepower per set.

MORE ZEPHYRS

Accordingly, the "Q's" board of directors in December 1935 authorized AFE #28270 in the amount of $2.25 million for two Shotwelded stainless steel 10-car trains including full dining, parlor and sleeping car space and twin stainless steel diesel-electric locomotives totaling 3,000 hp for power.

Budd completed the Denver Zephyr sets in early October of 1936. Each consist had 102 coach seats, 93 sleeping car accommodations of various designs, 10 parlor cars seats, and 104 non-revenue lounge and dining seats. The equipment was semi-articulated, with three cars free standing, while the remaining ones were articulated into two groups of two, and one group of three. The Denver Zephyr, including locomotives, was an impressive 883 feet 9 inches of gleaming stainless steel. In 1938 a combination 16-seat dinette/40-seat-coach was added to each equipment set followed by a 21-bed sleeper the next year stretching the Denver Zephyr to an impressive 12-car length and 274 revenue coach, parlor or sleeping car spaces.

When the #9906-led Denver Zephyr set passed Belmont, Illinois inbound for Chicago at 8:12 a.m. on November 5, 1939 the stainless steel Zephyr fleet marked its 8 millionth mile

The Zephyr in miniature:

Toy train manufacturers in 1934 raced to help Santa fill many a boy's wish for a miniature Zephyr under the family Christmas tree.

First to get models to market were the American Flyer Manufacturing Company of Chicago and Western Coil & Electric Company of Racine, Wisconsin. Toy train giant Lionel was already involved in producing a copy of the recently delivered—October 2, 1934—Union Pacific's M-10001, City of Portland, and did not have a Zephyr-style train for the 1934 Christmas season.

American Flyer was a well-known toy train manufacturer, the largest in the Midwest, and second only to Lionel. It worked closely with the Burlington and Budd for preliminary drawings and even managed to have CB&Q Zephyr Pilot Jack Ford appear at numerous department store Toylands shortly before Christmas, 1934: New York-12/13; Boston-12/14; Baltimore-12/17; Washington DC-12/18; Pittsburgh-12/19; Buffalo-12/20; Cleveland-12/21; Detroit-12/22; and St. Louis-12/23.

400 ZEPHYR SETS

Based upon American Flyer's preliminary design in the spring/summer of 1934, the CB&Q board of directors authorized the purchase of 400 sets of AF Zephyrs, so one could be in operation in all CB&Q stations when the prototype Zephyr went into service on November 11, 1934. American Flyer also got another volume order for 200 sets, so that all across America Zephyrs could be seen streaking around in a circle inside every theatre lobby where *Silver Streak* was playing.

Ultimately the American Flyer Zephyrs did not sell well to the general public. Some of this was the price; at $17.50 including three-car train, 8 curved and 6 straight tracks, and a 50-watt transformer, the price equaled an average workman's weekly wage. The quality of the aluminum sand casting of the three carbodies also varied, and the train was perhaps top heavy, derailing easily on tight radius tinplate track curves.

Beginning in 1935 American Flyer also produced Zephyr sets of lithographed sheet metal, which subsequently sold much better than the cast aluminum versions. At $6 for the electric set and $1.50 for the wind-up one, it's no wonder they were more popular.

Also available to the general public for Christmas 1934 were Zephyr sets manufactured by Western Coil & Electric Company, a manufacturer of high quality electrical equipment. Western Coil & Electric had been selling its Tru-Trak line of wooden ties and extruded aluminum rails with moderate success over the past several years to O scale hobbyists, and decided to expand its presence in the toy train field with a Zephyr.

Unfortunately, Western Coil & Electric's management decided to make its Zephyr full 17/64" scale in width and height, including true articulation, which its AF competi-tion lacked, but foreshorten it substantially in length so it could run on the sharp curves of other manufacturers' O gauge track. The result pleased no one, being too short to be accepted by O scale hobbyists, and at $34 much too expensive for the children's play toy market.

LACKLUSTER SALES

The Western Coil & Electric Zephyr remained on the Midwest market through the late 1930's. Sales were so lackluster that some were even offered as kits with markings for either the Zephyr or the Boston & Maine/Maine Central Flying Yankee.

In 1935 Lionel entered the toy Zephyr market. However, since on April 4, 1935 the Boston & Maine/Maine Central railroads had introduced "the first streamlined train east of the Mississippi" in Boston, Mass.-Portland-Bangor, Maine service, that train was what Lionel chose to copy in O gauge (but not in true 1/4"-to-the-foot scale).

With selective compression used in creating the chrome-plated sheet metal car bodies, and offered in a price range between $7.50 (a three-car department store special without track or transformer) and $15.78 (including track, transformer and "remote" whistle) Lionel immediately garnered the majority of the 1935 Christmas toy train market. Lionel's Flying Yankee—in either three-or four-car sets—remained a catalog staple until wartime 1942. Lionel planned to offer it as the Victory Streamliner in blue with red and white trim for Christmas, 1942, but the War Production Board didn't cooperate.

Of course, throughout the streamline craze of the late 1930's numerous toy trains were introduced in either the Zephyr or Union Pacific "City" motifs. Well-known toy firms such as MARX produced both inexpensive clockwork ("wind-up") and electric trains, as did lesser-known manufacturers such as Hoge.

Streamline toy train interest lasted well into the postwar era. The moniker "Silver Streak" even appeared on an all-silver-finished American Flyer three-car passenger set in 1952. The set at $49.50 "East of Denver" and $51.00 "Denver & West" was in AF's upper price range. Chicago-based American Flyer had been purchased by toy maker giant A. C. Gilbert and moved to its New Haven, Connecticut headquarters in 1938.

Regardless of manufacturer, toy Zephyrs and other miniature streamliners by the tens-of-thousands circled America's Christmas trees and "Living Room Central Railroads" throughout the 1930's, '40's and '50's. They remain today as both valuable collector's items and priceless mementos of aging grandparents from a time when streamline trains fascinated—even beguiled—millions of American boys, and more than a few girls as well!

Twin girls, Marion and Frances Beeler, chisten the Twin Zephyrs in Chicago's Union Station on April 15, 1935. These trains entered service April 21 with passenger seating for 88; 64 in coach and 24 in the solarium-observation area of the train.

of revenue service. This amazing achievement occurred six days prior to the Pioneer Zephyr marking but its 5th anniversary in service.

In later years John Harbeson reminisced that the Denver Zephyr was his favorite passenger train design project. In company with the original Zephyr and the Santa Fe's 1937 Super Chief, that was high praise indeed. He also recalled with a smile that his senior associate, Paul Cret, was so well known in the late 1930's for innovative passenger car interior designs that architect Frank Lloyd Wright once commented, "He can shake them out of his sleeve!"

'SILVER' PREFIX

The Denver Zephyrs introduced the use of the "Silver" prefix on all future Burlington Route stainless steel passenger cars (except the Chicago-Twin Cities Train of the Gods and Train of the Goddesses which was delivered just weeks after the Denver Zephyr).

When the Denver Zephyr sets arrived in the Chicago area, behind steam, incidentally, EMC was still completing and testing locomotives #9906AB (Silver King/Queen) and #9907 AB (Silver Knight/Princess). The locomotives had two

Winton V-12 Model 201A engines rated at 900 hp each in the "A", or cab unit, and a single V-16 rated at 1,200 hp in the trailing, or "B" unit, for a total rating of 3,000 hp.

One of the few derogatory comments Ralph Budd received regarding the Denver to Chicago speed run of May 26, 1934 was from Daniel Willard, president of the Baltimore & Ohio RR. He belittled the remarkable accomplishment by claiming "it was all downhill from a mile high mountain." Never mind that the mountain was the equivalent of one end of a 10' board being held 1/8" off the ground.

Ralph Budd's response to the B&O's executive's challenge was succinct and memorable.

On Friday morning October 23, 1936 a specially shortened (sans four sleeping cars) six-car Denver Zephyr left Union Station Chicago exactly at 7:00 a.m. Locomotives #9906AB headed up the invitation-only "Gentlemen's Adventure" sponsored by the CB&Q and the Chicago Association of Commerce. Twelve hours, twelve minutes, and 27 seconds later the special drew to a halt 1,017 miles distant in Denver's Union Station. A top speed of 116 mph had been reached near Brush, Colorado and the fastest average speed between stations was for 6.11 miles at a scorching 107.3 mph. A new rail speed record—uphill, if

Posed side by side for a publicity photo on May 25, 1954, the four-car, 600 hp Pioneer Zephyr and the five-car streamlined Kansas City Zephyr, led by two 2,250 hp E-8 locomotives, are near Brookfield, Missouri. The Kansas City Zephyr featured two vista-dome cars.

you will—of 83.33 mph was set, one destined to stand for decades.

CHRISTEN DENVER ZEPHYR

On Saturday the four new sleepers—which had previously been moved to Denver—were attached to the consist. In early evening the now 10-car Denver Zephyr was christened with a bottle of Paul Garrett Special Champagne by Ms. Jane Garlow, the granddaughter of Buffalo Bill Cody, from astride her horse no less, and the Denver Zephyr roared eastbound out of town. It subsequently cruised at 95 mph, hit 105 mph, and arrived in Chicago Sunday morning, October 25, 1936 just two minutes behind the three-car Advanced Denver Zephyr's then current 15 hour, 50 minute schedule.

Denver Zephyr service started on November 8, 1936 with the christening by Jane Garlow in Chicago of the equipment set led by #9907, and the Union Pacific's City of Denver had serious competition. "Overnight, Every Night" became the standard of transportation between the two cities for the next three decades. Only the arrival of the even speedier—but hardly as luxurious—jet airliners and the always-convenient Interstate could empty the Denver Zephyrs.

The Burlington's new Twin Zephyrs arrived in Chicago from

Budd on December 14, 1936. Each set of equipment contained 120 coach seats, 43 parlor car seats and a three-person drawing room. Non-revenue space included 10 seats in the observation lounge, and 32 more in both the cocktail lounge and the dining car. The single locomotive (#9904-Pegasus, or #9905-Zephyrus) was rated at 1,800 hp from two Winton Model 201A V-12 engines. In concert with the locomotives, all cars were named for Greek or Roman mythological figures.

Promoted as the Train of the Gods and the Train of the Goddesses, they entered Twin City to Chicago revenue service on December 18, 1936. Soon, however, the public simply referred to them as the Morning or Afternoon Zephyr, as each set made a daily roundtrip. For years the Morning and Afternoon Zephyrs were two of America's fastest trains.

Their three-car predecessors were immediately reassigned. CB&Q #9901 initiated Sam Houston Zephyr service between Houston and Fort Worth, Texas, while #9902 began Ozark State Zephyr service between St. Louis and Kansas City, Missouri.

In 1937 a 16-seat dinette/40-seat chair car was added to each of the articulated Trains of the Gods and Goddesses making them eight cars long (including locomotives), with seating for 160 coach passengers, and a dining car capacity of 48.

The new diesel-electric locomotives of the Twin and Denver Zephyrs were not without problems. For backup service Electro-Motive supplied the Burlington with a prototype locomotive to substitute when needed on both Zephyr assignments. EMC #511 was similar in performance, but not carbody design, to the #9904, -05, -06A and 9907A. The "Q" formally leased the #511 from July 1936 through May 1937 when Aeolus was completed. What was Aeolus, you ask?

THE Q's AEOLUS

On April 11, 1937 the "Q's" West Burlington shops released upgraded Hudson-type 4-6-4 steam locomotive #4000 complete with a streamlined stainless steel shroud. In harmony with the car names of the Trains of the Gods and Goddesses, the locomotive was named Aeolus (Keeper of the Winds), but to the crews #4000 was "Big Alice the Goon!" Big Alice was successful enough that a second streamlined Hudson, #4001, was completed in February of 1938.

Between September 25 and October 9, 1938 #9904 (Pegasus) replaced #9906A (Silver Knight) in Denver Zephyr service while the #9906A had both diesel engines replaced at Electro-Motive. To substitute for #9904 EMC supplied brand new model E3A demonstrator #822, the first locomotive containing all EMC-built mechanical and electrical equipment. With its round reinforced nose and high setback automobile-like cab, operating crews and management alike were impressed with the new design.

The General Pershing Zephyr, introduced on April 20, 1939, replaced the Ozark State Zephyr—#9902 and its three-car articulated consist—on daily roundtrip service between St. Louis and Kansas City, Missouri. The General Pershing Zephyr was led by baggage car/locomotive #9908 constructed of stainless steel with a shovelnose front end and a 1,000 hp V-12 engine.

Although the slanted shovelnose was familiar, this final shovelnose locomotive introduced two new items to the Burlington: Electro-Motive's model 567 diesel engine, and the 14' 6" wheelbase A-1-A passenger truck created by EMC's brilliant designer, Martin Blomberg. The Electro-Motive 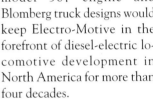 model 567 engine and Blomberg truck designs would keep Electro-Motive in the forefront of diesel-electric locomotive development in North America for more than four decades.

ARTICULATION GONE

With the General Pershing Zephyr the Burlington Route gave up on articulated design. The power car plus three-passenger car train set was comprised of four separable pieces of equipment, all equipped with two trucks each. Articulation's lack of flexibility was ultimately a higher price to pay than the savings predicted by its theoretical advantages with speed and reduced maintenance costs.

At West Hinsdale, Illinois the 4-6-4 Burlington streamlined Aeolus hauls the Ak-Sar-Ben's standard consist on the track at left, while the six-car Twin Zephyr occupies the middle track on November 8, 1933.

At West Quincy, Missouri in 1953, the Mark Twain Zephyr pulls into the station with snow on its nose and a large oscillating Mars light atop the headlight. To help streamline the roof line, the exhaust manifold and roof radiators were suspended from the roof frame inside the engine room. The power car was named Injun Joe. *Philip Weibler*

CB&Q #9908 was the last of the shovelnose Zephyr power cars, the slanted front end design having fallen out of favor thanks to lack of adequate collision protection for the headend crew as well as the problem of "sleeper flicker" caused by high speed and the hypnotic effect of crossties (known as sleepers in England) furiously passing under the nose.

In February of 1940 the Burlington received the first four of 16 "off the shelf" but stainless steel-clad, EMC model E5A/B 2000 hp passenger locomotives to power its expanding non-articulated Zephyr fleet. In all but exterior finish the locomotives were duplicates of EMC E3A #833, which had demonstrated on the road 18 months earlier.

The pre-WWII Zephyr fleet reached its limit with the addition of Texas Zephyr, Silver Streak Zephyr and Ak-Sar-Ben Zephyr services in 1940-41.

Business was booming.

After the war new trains and services were introduced, including that sublime passenger car creation, the dome car. The articulated sets, Train of the Gods and Train of the Goddesses were replaced with new Budd-built stainless steel streamlined individual cars in Twin Cities-Chicago service. After cleaning and sprucing up, the Train of the Gods and Train of the Goddesses became the Nebraska Zephyrs, and

one set remains preserved in operable condition at the Illinois Railroad Museum in Union, Illinois today.

CALIFORNIA ZEPHYR

On March 20, 1949 the Burlington Route, in concert with the Denver, Rio Grande Western and Western Pacific railroads, introduced the incomparable California Zephyr, an 11-car, five-dome car luxury train of six equipment sets to extend daily Zephyr service from Chicago to San Francisco (actually Oakland) via Denver, the Moffat Tunnel, Salt Lake City, and the Feather River Canyon. It was arguably Budd's and the Burlington's finest creation.

A stainless steel reprise came in October of 1956 when the "Q" placed in service two new non-articulated Denver Zephyr sets led by twin EMD 2400 hp E-9 model locomotives. The equipment would roll on "overnight every night" until May 1, 1971, and Budd's Shotwelded stainless steel equipment—from the Burlington and many other roads—would then soldier on for two more decades in Amtrak service well into the 1990's.

What started with stainless steel, a "very nervy railroad president," and "moderne stream-line design" turned out very well indeed for the Burlington Route and its patrons between the mid-1930's and the mid-1960's.

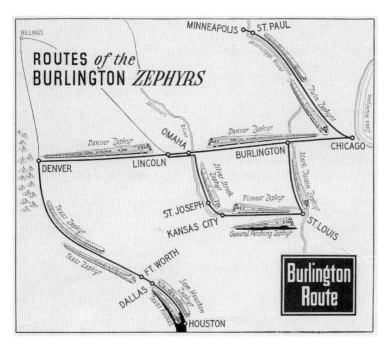

CB&Q Zephyr routes in 1940.

The Chicago Association of Commerce issued this invitation for October 23–24, 1936 for the speed run between Chicago and Denver of the new Denver Zephyr.

"Whoof" went Burlington's Mark Twain Zephyr across Nebraska when it set a new world's record of 122 miles per hour. Engineer Jack Ford (inset) was at the controls. Photo is personally signed and dated by Jack Ford. *Chris Burritt collection*

Success Unbounded

The success of the Zephyr created a world of new business opportunities for Budd, Electro-Motive and Winton Engine.

By mid-1935 Budd had orders for stainless steel trains that its Hunting Park plant would take months to produce. In January 1936, Budd released Santa Fe #3070, the world's first full-sized lightweight (41 3/4 tons) stainless steel passenger car. Budd-built streamliners produced in 1937 alone included Reading's Crusader for twice-daily service between New York City (Jersey City, New Jersey) and Philadelphia, the Rock Island's six Rockets across the granger road's Midwest lines from Chicago to Texas, and of course the Santa Fe's majestic "Train of the Stars," its original all-Pullman Super Chief on ATSF's Chicago to Los Angeles route. Its extra fare coach-only brethren, the El Capitan, followed in February 1938 and signaled the development of a new passenger train concept, the extra fare, fast, but coach-only streamliner. Seaboard Air Line introduced a similar overnight coach streamliner, the Silver Meteor, in February 1939 for New York to Florida service and competitor Atlantic Coast Line's Champion arrived from Budd that December.

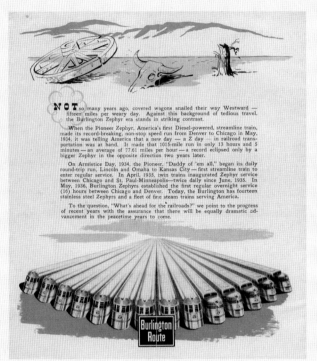

NOT so many years ago, covered wagons snailed their way Westward — fifteen miles per weary day. Against this background of tedious travel, the Burlington Zephyr era stands in striking contrast.

When the Pioneer Zephyr, America's first Diesel-powered, streamline train, made its record-breaking, non-stop speed run from Denver to Chicago in May, 1934, it was telling America that a new day — a Z day — in railroad transportation was at hand. It made that 1015-mile run in only 13 hours and 5 minutes — an average of 77.61 miles per hour — a record eclipsed only by a bigger Zephyr in the opposite direction two years later.

On Armistice Day, 1934, the Pioneer, "Daddy of 'em all," began its daily round-trip run, Lincoln and Omaha to Kansas City — first streamline train to enter regular service. In April, 1935, twin trains inaugurated Zephyr service between Chicago and St. Paul-Minneapolis—twice daily since June, 1935. In May, 1936, Burlington Zephyrs established the first regular overnight service (16) hours between Chicago and Denver. Today, the Burlington has fourteen stainless steel Zephyrs and a fleet of fine steam trains serving America.

To the question, "What's ahead for the railroads?" we point to the progress of recent years with the assurance that there will be equally dramatic advancement in the peacetime years to come.

PEARL HARBOR

The brisk business in new streamliners continued through the introduction of Budd's stainless steel streamlined but steam-powered New York Central Empire State Limited on Sunday, December 7, 1941. The gala affair was tragically upstaged by the Japanese attack on Pearl Harbor and streamliner construction stopped "for the duration."

In 1943 Budd moved to a new U.S. Government-built war contract work plant in the Philadelphia suburb of Red Lion. The Budd Railway and Highway Trailer Divisions moved to Red Lion in 1946, Budd bought the facility in 1948, and all of Budd's postwar streamliners were conceived and created therein. Thousands of transit cars for New York, Chicago, and other cities were also Shotwelded together at Red Lion through the 1970's.

Caught in erratic sales in the 1970's and the merger mania of the 1980's, Budd was sold and resold. However, the files, photo archives, and patents rights of the Budd Company Railcar Division today reside in Philadelphia as part of the multi-national Bombardier Corp., whose stainless steel commuter rail cars are in service across North America and are still being fabricated to-

day. Ironically, Bombardier also holds the manufacturing and patent rights to passenger car designs of Pullman-Standard, Budd's main competitor!

The 660 horsepower of that Winton diesel engine propelled both Winton and Electro-Motive into the forefront of powering the new streamliners flashing across America. Electro-Motive built a manufacturing facility in the Chicago suburb of McCook (with a mailing address of LaGrange) in 1935-36, and the first of its majestic slanted nose, 70-feet long, six-axle streamline Model E passenger locomotives rolled out of the erecting bay in May of 1937. Orders continuously arrived for motive power to lead the new fleets of Budd and Pullman-Standard streamliners under construction.

Winton Engine's locomotive applications were transferred to Electro-Motive in 1936, and Winton was reorganized as GM's Cleveland Engine Division in 1937. It remained in business as a marine and stationary engine supplier until the early 1960's.

DIESELS REPLACE STEAM

Electro-Motive introduced its first freight locomotive in 1939, became a GM Division (EMD) in 1941, and spent the next two decades putting the steam locomotive and its builders out of business. Some years in the 1950's and '60's EMD had more than 80% of all diesel locomotive orders in North America. U.S. main line steam operations ceased in 1960, and Canada followed in 1961.

The railroad merger movement of the 1980's plus aggressive competition from General Electric resulted in EMD having a much reduced market by the early 1990's, when it closed and demolished two-thirds of its storied LaGrange facility. Today engines and components are still manufactured at LaGrange, but are then shipped to London, Ontario, Canada for assembly into completed locomotives.

Although the railroad industry has changed dramatically since 1934, the majority of locomotives in North America today still trace their heritage directly back to that modest Winton diesel engine supplied by little EMC in the 1934 Pioneer Zephyr.

The Museum of Science and Industry in Chicago and the Smithsonian Institution of Washington D.C. are worthy and appropriate repositories of the tangible remnants from one of the great social and transportation revolutions in history.

ABOVE. The gleaming 12-car Denver Zephyr was propelled by 1,800 horsepower from a pair of EMC/Winton V-12 201-A engines in the lead locomotive and a 1,200 hp V-16 in the booster for a total of 3,000 hp. The train had a full size diner seating 40 people. BELOW. Nighttime view of Twin Zephyr billboard in Chicago.

THE ZEPHYR

Views on this page and the previous page show Burlington Zephyr advertising billboards, as well as views of the Pioneer Zephyr (top), and (below) the much longer 12-car Denver Zephyr.

ABOVE. This Zephyr float won first prize of $50 in a Denver parade in October of 1937, celebrating the opening of the West 8th Avenue Viaduct. Four Kappa Delta sorority sisters rode on the float, two on each side. BELOW. This nearly identical Burlington float was part of the Winter Sports Parade in January 1940 in Denver.

The booklet "The California Zephyr" produced by Burlington shows that train with vista-dome cars, traveling through high mountains. The California Zephyr featured hostesses called Zephyrettes.

These two photos show the Pioneer Zephyr making its last run on March 20, 1960 at Lincoln, Nebraska (right) and at Omaha. The Pioneer Zephyr had marked its 25th anniversary in regular passenger service on November 11, 1959. On May 26, 1960, the Zephyr was donated by the Burlington Railroad to the Museum of Science and Industry. *Both photos, Dick Rumbolz, Charles Zeiler collection*

The Nebraska Zephyr, which began service in 1947, was actually a reincarnation of the 1936 Twin Zephyrs.The westbound train left Chicago at 12:45 p.m. and arrived in Lincoln, Nebraska at 10:30 p.m. that evening. Eastbound, the train left Lincoln at 11 a.m. and arrived in Chicago at 8:45 p.m.

THE NEBRASKA ZEPHYR...DAILY BETWEEN CHICAGO, OMAHA AND LINCOLN

The Twin Zephyrs ran between Chicago and St. Paul/Minneapolis, with service starting on April 21, 1935. These second, longer train sets were built by Budd, powered by EMC, featured articulated cars, and entered service on December 18, 1936.

HERITAGE FROM THE GODS
BURLINGTON'S *new 8 car* TWIN ZEPHYRS

The Denver Zephyr began service on November 8, 1936 and only some of its cars were articulated. Each car in the train was named. The train's promotional material read "Overnight-Everynight," and "A Travel Triumph of Beauty, Comfort, Convenience..."

OVERNIGHT · EVERYNIGHT

Burlington's DENVER ZEPHYR

BETWEEN CHICAGO AND DENVER

Mark Twain Zephyr along the Mississippi, Quincy, Illinois

LEFT. The four-car Mark Twain Zephyr, first operated on October 28, 1935, zips along the Mississippi River near Quincy, Illinois. The articulated train featured power unit #9903 and a rounded observation car with the signature and picture of Mark Twain at the rear as a tailsign. *Don Heimburger collection*

The most famous Zephyr after the Pioneer Zephyr was the California Zephyr, jointly operated by the Burlington, the Rio Grande and the Western Pacific. It offered a two-night run between Chicago and San Francisco (Oakland). CZ cars from the Budd Company began arriving in 1948, and some cars were used on the Exposition Flyer until the entire fleet of CZ cars had arrived. The California Zephyr was noted for its five vista-dome cars in the train consist. *Don Heimburger collection*

The Burlington knew that their streamlined Zephyr locomotives would need periodic maintenance and would thus be out of service occasionally. The railroad streamlined two S-4 Class 4-6-4 locomotives and named them Aeolus, Keeper of the Winds in Greek mythology. The locomotives were used on the Twin Zephyrs and the Denver Zephyr. *Don Heimburger collection*

The 1,800 hp A unit Silver King was one of EMC's first non-articulated single-ended locomotives. Here it is shown right after it was completed at the EMC plant in October of 1936. *Don Heimburger collection*

ABOVE AND BELOW. In October, 1936, one of the Denver Zephyrs set a world's record for a long-distance non-stop run between Chicago and Denver at an average speed of more than 83 miles an hour. The Denver Zephyrs achieved amazing on-time performance records. *Both photos, Don Heimburger collection*

ABOVE. This view shows the Twin Cities Zephyr rushing past a railroad crossing as a group of people look on, enjoying the passing of the train and probably wishing they were on it. *Bombardier, Don Heimburger collection* BELOW. The AIA Blomberg power truck (at lower right) was a distinguishing mark of the new General Pershing Zephyr power car. The St. Louis to Kansas City service was inaugurated on April 30, 1939 in St. Louis. Ralph Budd is at the microphone. *Bombardier, Don Heimburger collection*

Epilogue

— The Zephyr today —
Retirement & Digital Rebirth

The date of May 26, 1960 found the Pioneer Zephyr sitting on a short length of track beside Chicago's Museum of Science and Industry. After the requisite speeches and visits from old friends such as Jack Ford, the Pioneer Zephyr settled down to a peaceful slumber beside captured WWII German submarine U-505.

It is appropriate—but only co-incidental—that the German U-boat and the middle car of the Pioneer Zephyr share the same unit identification number—U-505. After all, the two technologies share common roots, as both U.S. and German WWI submarine power plants were developed from Herr Diesel's original designs, and the desire by the U.S. Navy in the early 1930's to improve upon them helped General Motors/Winton justify the development costs of their two-stroke cycle diesel prime mover.

WINTON POWER

Indeed, it was 1,300 hp Winton V-16 prime movers—built concurrently with the 8-cylinder engines for the Pioneer Zephyr, Flying Yankee and Twin Cities Zephyrs—that powered America's first seven WWII-era submarines assembled in 1934-35.

For its 50th birthday party in 1984 the Pioneer Zephyr was moved slightly by the Museum, but otherwise remained closed, and viewed by the general public only from the exterior. Although cleaned up and painted by Aurora shops before its donation to the Museum in 1960, by the mid-1980s the Zephyr was tired, weatherworn and deteriorating.

In the early 1990's the Museum's Board of Trustees approved an ambitious expansion plan including the construction of a new wing to the museum and an underground parking garage. Since both the Zephyr and U-505 would have to be moved for the construction, it was decided that both deteriorating exhibits would be completely cosmetically restored

On display outside at the Museum of Science and Industry, the Pioneer Zephyr sat on a 200-foot length of track in May of 1960.

and ensconced within the new construction.

The famous Pioneer Zephyr's new home would be the building's new spacious Great Hall.

In October of 1994 the Pioneer Zephyr was disassembled, and its three sections were transferred from its articulated trucks onto specially constructed dual-wheeled dollies. The dollies and their stainless steel cargo, looking like some giant's misplaced rubber-tired pull toy, were then moved via rigger Big Red Machinery Movers to the shops of Northern Railcar in Milwaukee. There the three-year restoration began.

Paint, flooring, wall and ceiling paneling, seats, carpeting, you name it, was removed, catalogued, repaired if possible, and if not, replaced with as close to an identical piece of material as could be found or fabricated. At one point the Zephyr looked much like it did in early 1934 at Budd's Hunting Park plant when it consisted of stainless steel frames on blocks and little else. All steps in the restoration were meticulously documented and photographed.

REFURBISHING COMPLETE

On September 7, 1997 the Zephyr stood gleaming and completed at Northern Railcar. The following morning a crew of 10 men was assembled—in honor of those long dead Budd company employees of April 7, 1934—and with great effort and a modicum of fanfare the sparkling stainless steel Zephyr once again rolled into sunlight.

Once clear of the shop and ready for disassembly into its three sections, each Zephyr section was wrapped in blue protective plastic, the ultimate "bag" job!

In early October of 1997 the Zephyr left Northern Railcar via rigger Big Red Machinery Movers for its return to the Museum of Science and Industry. On the way from Milwau-

Volunteers help spruce up the Pioneer Zephyr circa 1984, which was displayed at the Museum on a 200-foot length of track next to a German submarine U-505. Both Zephyr and submarine have now been moved indoors.

kee to Chicago the carefully-wrapped Zephyr stopped at the W. W. Grainger Company of Skokie, Illinois. The Grainger Foundation, under control of W. W. Grainger President David Grainger, who is a member of the Museum of Science and Industry's Board of Directors, had contributed the majority of the funds for the train's $1.5 million restoration.

Zephyr Draws Crowd

To say "Thank You" the Zephyr spent October 12 at Grainger's Skokie, Illinois headquarters so employees and guests could have a close-up view. The 63-year-old silvery streamliner still could—and quickly did—draw a crowd of admirers.

What changes had been wrought at the Museum of Science and Industry during the Zephyr's absence. A giant concrete basement 40 feet deep, 268 feet wide and 625 feet long now stood near where the Zephyr had formerly resided. A 200-foot length of ballasted track was laid on the concrete floor, and the steel trucks of the Zephyr were placed on the track.

One by one on October 16 and 17, 1997 each Zephyr section was carefully lifted by a huge Manitowoc M-260 crane with a specially fabricated lifting jig, swung about, and lowered onto its respective trucks waiting on the tracks below.

With the Zephyr safely in place in its new, climate-controlled home, work continued apace on the new building expansion, and the 1,500-car parking garage surrounding the biggest vehicle in the new facility: the Pioneer Zephyr!

With great fanfare, news coverage, and remarks by Chicago Mayor Richard M. Daley, Museum President and CEO David R. Mosena; Museum Board of Trustee's Chairman W. James Farrell, and other notables, the Museum of Science and Industry opened its new wing, underground parking garage, and Pioneer Zephyr display on Thursday, July 16, 1998.

New Computer Graphics

In addition to all the renovations done internally and externally, the Museum used new computer graphics and animatronics to tell the story of the Pioneer Zephyr. As guests enter the train following a docent (guide) via the baggage area they meet "Zeph," the Colorado burro, who magically retells the story of his great speedy adventure, and even the most wiggly child is all ears when Zeph speaks!

The docent then continues with the story after seating the group of 15-20 visitors in the chair car seats of the Zephyr.

To permit the tour to conclude with an integrated digital presentation, all the windows in the observation lounge have been converted to flat screen digital monitors, and visitors appear to have accidentally intruded into the observation lounge where Ralph Budd and guests (mannequins) are enjoying the adventure of the Denver to Chicago speed run in "real time."

Animatronics include Mr. Budd and his guests speaking while the train clickety-clacks and rocks at realistic speed as the countryside flashes past from window to window. The "trip" is capped with the Zephyr, after completing the speed

Zephyr Arrives at Museum

America's first diesel-powered streamliner train, the Burlington Railroad's Pioneer Zephyr, was placed on permanent exhibition at the Museum of Science and Industry in Chicago today (Thursday, May 26).

Dedication ceremonies were held at the display site outdoors at the east end of the Museum, adjacent to the captured German submarine U-505, on the 26th anniversary of the Zephyr's historic 1,000-mile dawn-to-dusk run from Denver to Chicago, which set new speed and distance records for a non-stop trip.

Today's ceremonies were climaxed when Harry C. Murphy, president of the Burlington, presented the throttle of the Pioneer Zephyr to Major Lenox R. Lohr, president of the Museum.

In his remarks Mr. Murphy cited highlights of the non-stop run, while Major Lohr recalled that he had "accepted" the train twice before; first, when he was manager of the Century of Progress World Fair, whose opening in 1934 was signaled by the train's arrival from Denver, and again in 1949, when he was president of the Railroad Fair, where it also was exhibited.

Other participants in today's presentation ceremonies included Edward G. Budd, Jr., president of the Budd Company, builder of the stainless-steel train; B. B. Brownell, director of engineering and research for the Electro-Motive Division of General Motors Corporation, which developed the train's diesel engines; and several Burlington men who were on the dawn-to-dusk run.

The Pioneer Zephyr, resting on its own specially-constructed track, will be open to the public during the spring, summer, and early fall months each year. Visitors can walk through the full length of the train's three cars to see the lounge and coach sections, illuminated displays in the baggage section depicting events in its quarter century of service, the Railway Post Office section, and the 660-horsepower diesel-electric locomotive unit.
Museum of Science and Industry press release, 1960

ABOVE AND BELOW. These views show the Pioneer Zephyr from various angles. Above, the railway post office compartment displays the mail bags used to sort mail. The cab where the motorman operated the train is shown below.

The Zephyr coach featured indirect lighting, luggage racks (added after delivery) above the passenger seats, and large windows to soak in the view.

The solarium-observation was equipped with a small writing table and lamp, comfortable armchairs and ashtrays which are anchored to the floor. Passengers were treated to the best views from this car.

When the Zephyr arrived at the Museum, it had traveled 3,222,898 miles in its career. To reach the museum, the Zephyr was disassembled into its three sections, each of which was transported by lowboy truck from the Illinois Central team track at Hyde Park in Chicago to the Museum.

run, continuing on and entering the Century of Progress Exhibition grounds with its many illuminated displays visible out each window.

It is a superb restoration and interpretive historical presentation of which the Messieurs Budd would wholeheartedly approve. Missing only is the roar of that Winton Engine, an occasional bray from Zeph, and a $0.20 ham and cheese sandwich in the buffet!

Zephyr's Legacy Remains

Although ultimately derailed by the speed of the jet airliner and the convenience of the interstate highway, still the Pioneer Zephyr's legacy remains intact thanks to the virtual domination of the railroad industry by diesel-electric passenger and freight locomotives, the use of stainless steel fabrication in most commuter/suburban passenger rail cars and many transit cars, and the development of limited high-speed rail operations in the congested Northeast Corridor of the USA today.

The genius, engineering skill and product development found in the Pioneer Zephyr represents the best of the American spirit and "can do" optimism in response to economic depression and social despair.

The Pioneer Zephyr is in good hands, lovingly and meticulously restored, and ready and able to tell its story to yet another generation of Americans.

After its 3-year restoration, the trailblazing Pioneer Zephyr is hauled by manpower out of Northern Rail Car's shop in Milwaukee during a September 8, 1997 ceremony that recreates the train's original roll-out in 1934. NRC restored the historic diesel-powered streamliner for Chicago's Museum of Science and Industry, where it is a major exhibit located 40 feet below ground level in the Museum's Great Hall. The September roll-out, cut short because of threatening skies, may have been the last outdoor appearance of a fully assembled #9900; after the photo session, the train was taken off its wheelsets and trucked to Chicago for installation at the Museum in late October. The *Zephyr* exhibit opened in July of 1998. *Robert McGonigal, Kalmbach Publishing Company*

Zephyr Gleams in its New Museum Home

What may be the most dazzling—and effective—static rolling stock display in the nation is not in a railroad museum at all, but Chicago's Museum of Science and Industry. Opened on July 16, 1998 under the name "All Aboard the Silver Streak," the Burlington Route Pioneer Zephyr exhibit cost $4.8 million, of which $1.5 million went to restoring the train itself.

Located in the Museum's Great Hall, the Zephyr is visible to arriving visitors through windows that look down on its exhibit bay.

A high-level platform along one side enables one to step into the engineer's door to see the cab and engine room and to enter the RPO compartment, where an actor portraying a mail clerk addresses visitors from a translucent screen part way down the car. Sound effects and rocking motion give the impression of movement.

The core of the exhibit is a 20-minute tour of the rest of the train that details its May 26, 1934, Denver-Chicago nonstop run. Led by costumed docents, groups of 15-20 enter the storage-mail area at the rear of the lead car. In the baggage section of the second car, they find a talking, animatronic version of Zeph, the mule who rode the famous run.

Next, visitors walk through the car's buffet-grill and seating area to the coach section of the rear car. Re-corded voices from mannequins depicting various people (old engineer, salesman, reporter, etc.) advance the story of the dawn-to-dusk run. Seated among these characters, visitors feel like fellow passengers. The finale is the observation-lounge, in which an animatronic CB&Q President Ralph Budd speaks to two relatives.

Outside the train, display boards and short video programs deal with themes ranging from how diesel differs from steam to what it was like to run the Zephyr. Also provided are exhibits on aerodynamics, stainless steel, and—complete with a model of a Winton 201A engine—diesel-electric drive systems. Art deco home appliances show the popularity of streamlining.

Behind the observation car, stepped benches face a large video screen showing the train testing around Philadelphia, on its record run, and in later life. Also shown are the CB&Q's other Zephyrs, the Century of Progress fair, people relating Zephyr memories, and "Porky's Railroad," a hoot of an old cartoon featuring a new "Silver Fish" train.

Joe Schacter, head of the Museum's Zephyr project, says it has been a hit with visitors, who give it high marks. And it's getting its message across: Schacter says visitors waiting to tour the train scored an average of 0.4 on a 4.0-scale of Zephyr knowledge; those tested after the tour scored a near-perfect 3.9. *Robert McGonigal, Kalmbach Publishing Company*

The restored Pioneer Zephyr sees daylight again after an extensive overhaul in Milwaukee at Northern Railcar. The train was lifted into its new Museum quarters over several days. *Robert McGonigal*

With a giant red ribbon adorning the power car of the Pioneer Zephyr, the train is pulled out from the Northern Railcar shops, awaiting its transfer to Chicago and the Museum of Science and Industry. *Robert McGonigal*

The Pioneer Zephyr is now on exhibit at the Museum of Science and Industry in a portion of the 40 feet deep, 268 feet wide and 625 feet long parking structure opened in 1998. The train is on display in all its stainless steel splendor, as fresh and new as the day it was accepted by the Burlington Railroad on April 17, 1934. *Robert McGonigal*